MULTICULTURAL
ART ACTIVITIES

INTERMEDIATE

Editor:
Dona Herweck Rice

Editoral Director:
Sharon Coan

Art Direction:
Elayne Roberts

Cover Artist:
Bianco Nikki

Imaging:
Rick Chacón

Publishers:
Rachelle Cracchiolo
Mary Dupuy Smith

Author:
Betty Gaglio Cavanaugh

Illustrator:
Blanca Apodaca LaBounty, Sue Fullam,
and Agi Palinay

Teacher Created Materials, Inc.
P.O. Box 1040
Huntington Beach, CA 92647
©*1994 Teacher Created Materials, Inc.*
Made in U.S.A.

ISBN-1-55734-617-8

Table of Contents

African Art

*A*rt has been highly developed throughout Africa for thousands of years, and samples of African art can be found dating back to prehistoric times. Egyptian architecture, sculpture, and painting have long been studied and admired, and African art as a whole has gained great popularity in the western world throughout the twentieth century.

A basic principle of African art is the extreme simplification of figures coupled with such attention to details as ornamentation and color. Repeating geometric designs are also often used, showing force and vigor, and producing a sense of harmony and rhythm. The influence of such African techniques can be seen around the world. For example, early works of the famous Spanish artist, Pablo Picasso, demonstrate the exaggerated facial features and simplification of form which are characteristic of African art.

Activities

○ **Head Sculptures**

○ **Amulet Jewelry**

○ **Akan Akuaba Dolls**

○ **Ndebele Village**

○ **Kamban Decorated Calabash**

○ **Akan Adinkra Cloth**

○ **Masks**

Head Sculptures

W hile a figure in African art may be extremely simplified, careful attention is paid to the details of ornamentation and color. Supernatural beings are depicted by an overemphasis of the head, eyes, and hands. Enlarged eyes, noses, and mouths are created so that intelligent and truthful spirits may enter. In decoration, repeating geometric patterns are used to produce a sense of harmony and rhythm.

Materials:

- ❑ red clay
- ❑ toothpicks
- ❑ large paper clip
- ❑ paper to cover the work surface
- ❑ beads and wire (optional)

- ❑ tongue depressor
- ❑ water bowl
- ❑ paper plate
- ❑ kiln (if firing is desired)*

Procedures:

1. Roll the clay into a ball about the size of a baseball.
2. Hollow out the ball with the tongue depressor and place it on the paper plate.
3. Press two eye indentations into the clay with your thumb.
4. Sculpt a nose using the paper clip, or use extra clay to form the nose and then press the shape in place.
5. Shape the mouth area to form lips or an open mouth.
6. Smooth the sculpture with water.
7. Use clay to form other features such as ears or hair.
8. Use a toothpick to draw decorative designs on the clay.
9. After the sculpture has dried for about a week, fire in a kiln.
10. Beads may be added by stringing them on a wire or thread.

*Note: Several activities in this book require the use of a kiln. If no kiln is available, or if the use of a kiln is undesirable, dry the object naturally. In most cases, the effect will be passable, though firing is always better. See page 94 for more information about using a kiln and natural drying.

Amulet Jewelry

*G*ood luck charms are found in most civilizations and date back to the Stone Age. The purpose of these amulets is to protect against danger, sickness, or bad luck. They were worn suspended from a necklace by people throughout Africa as an ornamental part of their clothing. Materials used to create this jewelry were bone, wood, animal skins, teeth, shells, ivory, and metal. Each type of material was believed to contain special powers. For example, a pendant made from the teeth of a wild animal would protect the wearer from future attacks by that type of animal. Each necklace would have only one amulet that had a special meaning for the protection of the owner.

Materials:

- ❏ small leather pieces
- ❏ nails
- ❏ ruler
- ❏ feathers
- ❏ stones
- ❏ sample page (page 6); (for a necklace)
- ❏ string, or leather cord
- ❏ scissors
- ❏ glue
- ❏ beads
- ❏ shells
- ❏ thin wire
- ❏ yarn

Procedures:

1. Cut the leather into a rectangle shape.
2. Measure to find the center of one edge of the rectangle. Carefully make a hole large enough to thread the necklace.
3. Use a nail to carve lines into the leather. Designs should be simple geometric shapes and lines.
4. Attach other desired items to the amulet with glue or thin wire.
5. More holes can be made at the bottom edge of the pendant to dangle additional items.
6. For a necklace, braid yarn and thread it through the hole at the top of the amulet.

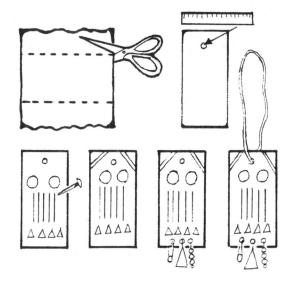

Variations:

1. *Clay:* Create the amulet from clay and use toothpicks to draw the designs. Clay beads can also be added. Fire the amulet in a kiln before threading it on the necklace.
2. *Cardboard:* Use brown corrugated cardboard from boxes to make the amulet shape. Various colors of construction paper can be added to create the designs.
3. *Stone:* Wrap a small colorful stone with thin copper wire to use as an amulet. Thread on a leather cord.

Amulet Jewelry: Sample Designs

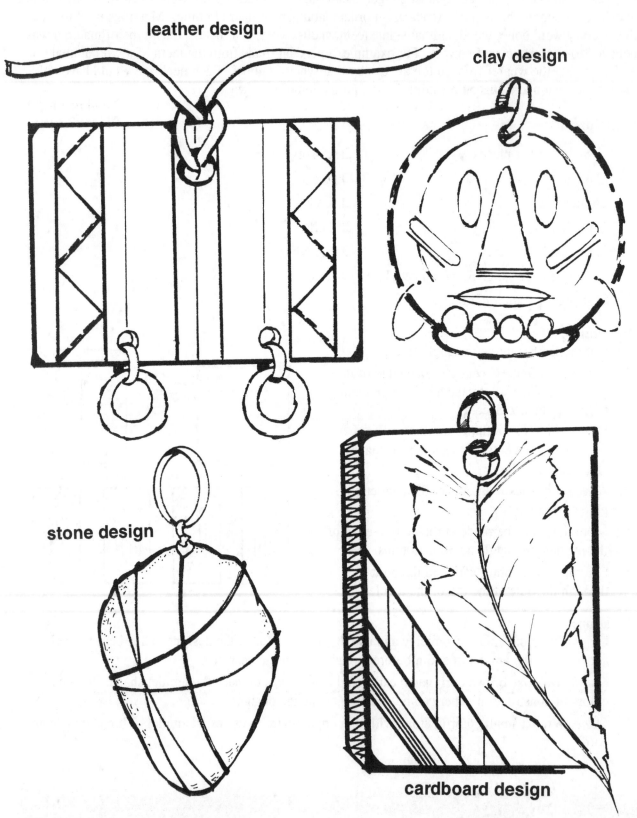

leather design

clay design

stone design

cardboard design

6

Akan Akuaba Dolls

A legend from the Akan people of Ghana tells about an unfortunate couple who had no children. The wife, Akua, went to their spiritual leader for advice. He gave her a beautiful doll made from clay that had a long, ringed neck and a large, decorated, oval head. Following the leader's instructions, Akua carried the doll with her always. Months later, she gave birth to a beautiful daughter.

Traditionally, men give the dolls to their wives, and the wives wear them in hopes of having beautiful children. Akan craftsmen make three styles of dolls. Those who desire a wise child will receive a doll that has a round head, called *Akuabatene*. Parents who want a boy child will receive a doll that has a rectangular head, called *Akuabanini*. Those who desire a girl will receive an *Akuababere* with an oval-shaped head.

These dolls are either carved from wood or formed out of clay. The head of the doll makes up half of the total figure. The body is narrow with short legs and arms outstretched at the sides. The Akuaba dolls have a shape similar to the ancient Egyptian ankh, or cross of life, and may have common origins.

Materials: clay, toothpick, rolling pin, plastic knife, dinner-sized paper plate, newspaper to cover work surface, water bowl, sample page (page 8), kiln (if firing is desired)

Procedures:
1. Roll the clay to form a thin slab about ½" (1.25 cm) thick.
2. Use a toothpick to draw the doll body lightly onto the surface of the clay. Mistakes can be removed easily by rubbing the clay with water.
3. Use a plastic knife to cut through the clay. Place the body shape flat onto the paper plate.
4. Smooth the edges of the body with water. Geometric designs and shapes may be added with additional clay or drawn with the toothpick.
5. After the clay has dried for a week, fire it in a kiln.

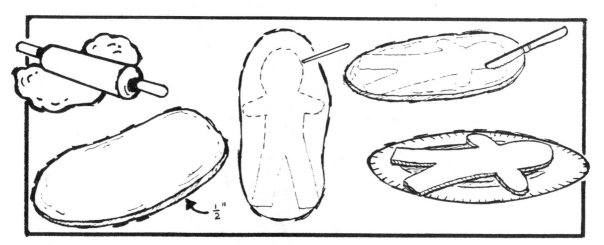

Variations:
1. *Necklace:* Tie ribbon or yarn around the neck of the doll to wear as a necklace for Mother's Day.
2. *Color:* Color may be added with ceramic glazes or acrylic paint.
3. *Paper:* Create the entire project from construction paper. Students may write their criteria for making their doll choice on the back of the doll.

Akan Akuaba Dolls: Sample Designs

Akuabatene

Akuabanini

Akuababere

Ndebele Village

*T*he Ndebele people migrated from the southeastern coast of Africa, settling in the Transvaal area in the seventeenth century. They became known for the beautifully decorated facades of their thatched-roof, mud houses. The settlements are a cluster of rectangular units linked by walls to create courtyard areas. The design and decoration of the settlements are influenced by Islamic house styles. The walls and floors are plastered smooth and dried to a rock-like hardness before being white-washed. Geometric lines and shapes create symmetrical patterns that are painted with colored clay. Bright, strong colors, such as red, yellow, green, and orange, are used to paint the designs on the front of the houses. Each shape is outlined in black. Enclosures for animals and unimportant areas, such as the back sides of the structures, are painted with beige and brown shapes.

Materials:

- ❑ heavy white drawing paper or poster board (2 pieces; 9" x 12" or 23 cm x 30 cm)
- ❑ construction paper in assorted colors
- ❑ scissors
- ❑ ruler
- ❑ pencil
- ❑ glue
- ❑ black marking pens or crayons with a wide point

Procedures:

1. Position the paper in a horizontal direction, and locate the center of the top edge. Draw a 4.5" (11 cm) line down from this center point (perpendicular to the top edge). Cut this line on each sheet of paper to make a slit.

2. By the cut, label one sheet A and the other B. Position paper A with the cut on the top and paper B with the cut on the bottom.

3. Draw a symmetrical roof line on the top edge of each sheet of paper. Cut on this line.

4. Slide the two slits together to interlock the papers. Form right angles to stand up the structure.

5. Cut geometric shapes from construction paper to create the designs for the structure. Carefully glue them in place, and then outline each shape in black when completed. Other lines may be added for decoration with the black pen.

6. Group the completed structures together to create several villages.

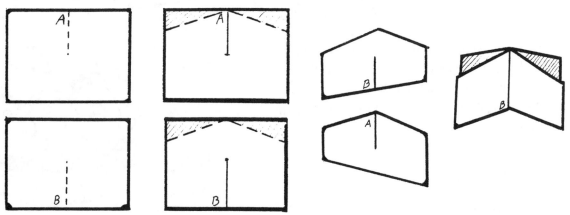

Kamban Decorated Calabash

A calabash is a hard-skinned gourd that is hollowed out to be used as a utensil. Among the Kamba people of Kenya, designs painted on a calabash represent a traditional art form. Items of special importance are made from the gourds and used for ceremonial occasions. Intricately carved or painted bowls, cups, spoons, and musical instruments are the most popular items.

Gourds are carefully grown and picked when their size and shape are needed for a particular purpose. The meat of the gourd is scraped out, and the rind is left to dry in the hot sun. After the calabash hardens, it is cut into the desired shape and then decorated. Three methods of decoration are used. The first is to stain the rind of the gourd with plant dyes. The second method is to paint geometric patterns on the outside of the calabash. The most intricate method is to carve or scrape the designs into the rind. Sometimes colorful beads or stones are pushed into the designs before the gourd completely hardens. Dye is used to highlight the carved patterns. Other elements of design used on the calabash are plants, animals, or scenes depicting favorite stories and legends.

Materials:
- ❏ pumpkin
- ❏ pencil
- ❏ nails
- ❏ push-pins
- ❏ hairpins
- ❏ diluted black tempera paint
- ❏ sponge or paintbrush
- ❏ newspaper to cover the work area
- ❏ beads and straight pins (optional)

Procedures:
1. Draw the design on the pumpkin rind with a pencil. Shapes and lines should have a lot of space between them.

2. Use push-pins to carve thin lines into the pumpkin rind. Follow the pencil marks as a guide. The nails and hairpins will create wide lines and can be used to scrape off specific areas in the design.

3. Carefully sponge or paint the carved areas with the diluted black tempera. Wipe the surface of the pumpkin clean.

4. Small beads can be attached to the rind with thin wire.

Akan Adinkra Cloth

*S*ometimes referred to as "saying good-bye cloth," Adinkra cloth is a colorful fabric print worn during elaborate funeral services and periods of mourning. Worn by the Akan tribe of West Africa, the cloth is an elegant form of dress used in celebrating the memory of the departed. Meaningful symbols that express the wearer's feelings toward the dead person cover the cloth. Some symbols represent poetic messages; others may illustrate comforting proverbs and sayings.

In Africa, Adinkra cloth can be purchased in the market place. Custom-made cloth can be ordered from an Adinkra printer. Usually six or eight different symbols are used; they are repeated in rows alternating with bold geometric shapes and repetitive patterns.

Students may use these techniques and designs to create a banner, head scarf, sash, or belt.

Materials:
- ❑ crayons
- ❑ muslin (or manila drawing paper)
- ❑ diluted brown tempera paint
- ❑ wide paintbrush (if using paper)
- ❑ symbols (page 12)

Procedures:

1. African designs are based on bold geometric shapes and repetitive lines. Use crayons to draw rows of Adinkra symbols along with geometric shapes. You may draw the symbols first with pencil. A heavy application of crayon then needs to be applied.

2. After the muslin is covered with the crayon designs, dip the entire cloth into a solution of diluted tempera paint. Squeeze the water from the cloth and lay it flat to dry.

3. If manila paper is used to create a banner, use a wide paintbrush to apply the diluted paint.

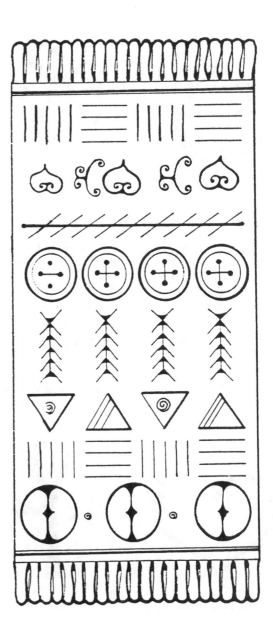

Akan Adinkra Cloth: Symbols

independence

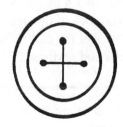

king of all symbols

hope

family history

law

jealousy

wisdom and knowledge

good luck

agreement

the first Adinkra symbol

forgiveness

royalty

patience and endurance

life

strength

praise

Masks

*M*asks are a very important element in African culture, and each has its own purpose. Some are ornamental while others are used in religious ceremonies or in elaborate rituals. Used by dancers, masks are a way of communicating with the various spirits. The spirits express themselves through the masks. The artists who construct these masks are highly regarded. Their knowledge of the supernatural enables them to carve masks which will house the spirit forces. A misconception is the idea that witch doctors scare evil spirit out of their patients. Instead, the doctors wear the masks to concentrate the healing powers of nature.

The masks are constructed from various materials. They are decorated with simple, strong, and powerful shapes and designs.

Materials:
- ❑ three sheets of brown, gray, black, white, or beige construction paper (12" x 18" or 30 cm x 45 cm)
- ❑ pencils
- ❑ scissors
- ❑ glue or stapler
- ❑ patterns (pages 14-15)

Procedures:
1. The mask should be limited to three colors: one for the face of the mask and two colors for facial features and decorations.
2. On one sheet of construction paper, draw a large egg shape or use the patterns provided.
3. Cut out the shape, and then cut a 1½" (4 cm) slit at the forehead, chin, and cheeks.
4. Overlap the sides of each slit and staple or glue together. This will make the mask three-dimensional.
5. Decorate the mask using geometric shapes, lines, and designs. The eyes, nose, and mouth should be exaggerated to show their importance.
6. **Optional:** Use raffia fibers or shredded corn husks for hair.

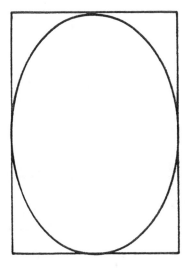 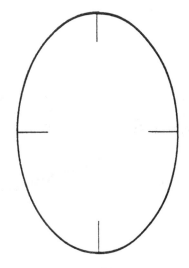 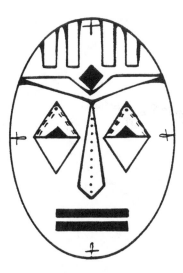

Mask Pattern (Top)

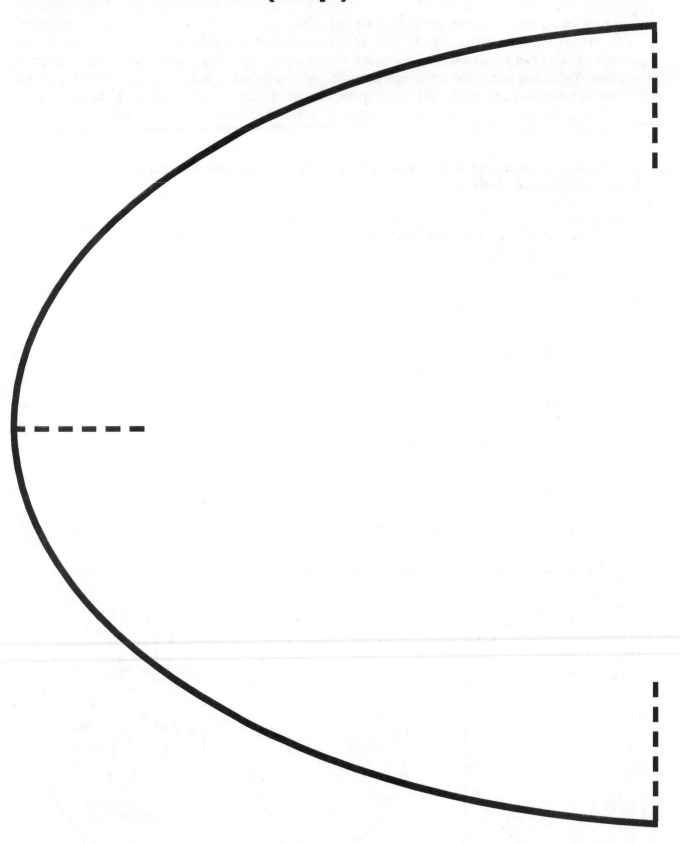

Mask Pattern (Bottom)

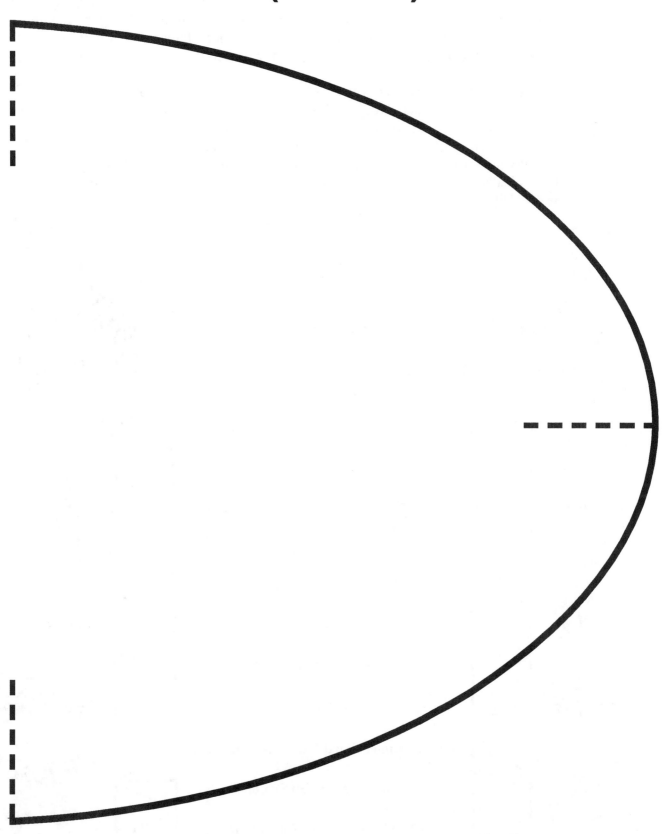

Native American Art

*T*he art of Native Americans is as diverse as it is beautiful. Naturally, it is reflective of the culture in which it has been created. As a general rule, the Native American art throughout history has attempted to make everyday objects not only functional but also attractive.

Historically, American Indians have worked with a variety of art forms. Pottery dates back for countless centuries, traditionally created through the coil method. Basket weaving, though primarily practical, also attracted the skills of master weavers who created beautifully feathered, beaded, and colored works of art. Weavers of cloth were so skilled that some of their fabrics cannot be improved upon by modern machinery, and Europeans of past centuries sometimes mistook their woven cloth for fine cotton fabric. Finally, painters and carvers have used their skills to create pieces that even today are treasured and widely copied.

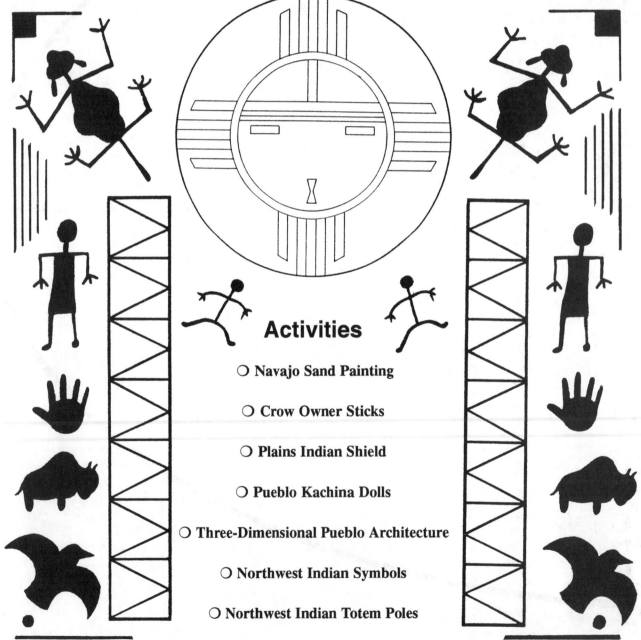

Activities

○ **Navajo Sand Painting**

○ **Crow Owner Sticks**

○ **Plains Indian Shield**

○ **Pueblo Kachina Dolls**

○ **Three-Dimensional Pueblo Architecture**

○ **Northwest Indian Symbols**

○ **Northwest Indian Totem Poles**

16

Navajo Sand Painting

*T*he Pueblo drew sacred designs on the floors of their kivas with dry, colored sand. These were the first Native American sand paintings. Navajo designs followed. They were the most elaborate and became a part of Navajo rituals. Sand paintings are made of symbolic pictures and used for healing ceremonies that deal with the harmony of life and nature. They are different for each ritual. Ceremonies that last for more than a day require a different sand painting for each day. After each ritual is complete, the paintings are destroyed. The designs are drawn from memory and are usually created by three or more people. Only the right hand is used to apply the colored sand onto the floor area. The symbols are begun in the center and are usually designed in a circle shape.

Materials:

- ❏ fine sandpaper
- ❏ crayons
- ❏ glue
- ❏ twine
- ❏ pencil
- ❏ cardboard (same size as sandpaper)
- ❏ drawing paper
- ❏ sample page (p. 18)

Procedures:

1. Sketch ideas for the sand painting on the drawing paper.
2. Select the best design, and carefully draw it on the sandpaper.
3. Glue the sandpaper to the cardboard.
4. Use crayon to color the design.
5. Optional: glue twine around the edges of the cardboard.

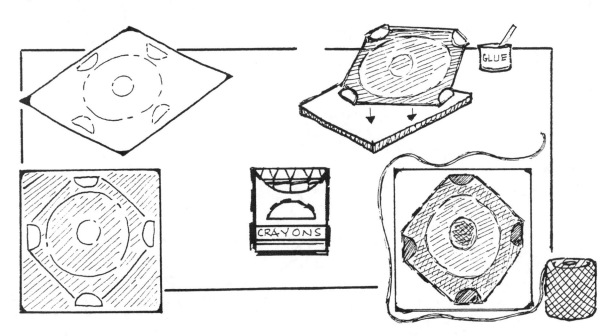

Fabric Variation:

Make a fabric banner using the crayon-colored sandpaper. Place the crayon side of the sand painting down on top of a piece of muslin or cotton fabric. Iron the back side of the sandpaper with the iron set at a medium to high temperature. The crayon design will appear on the fabric.

Navajo Sand Painting: Sample Designs

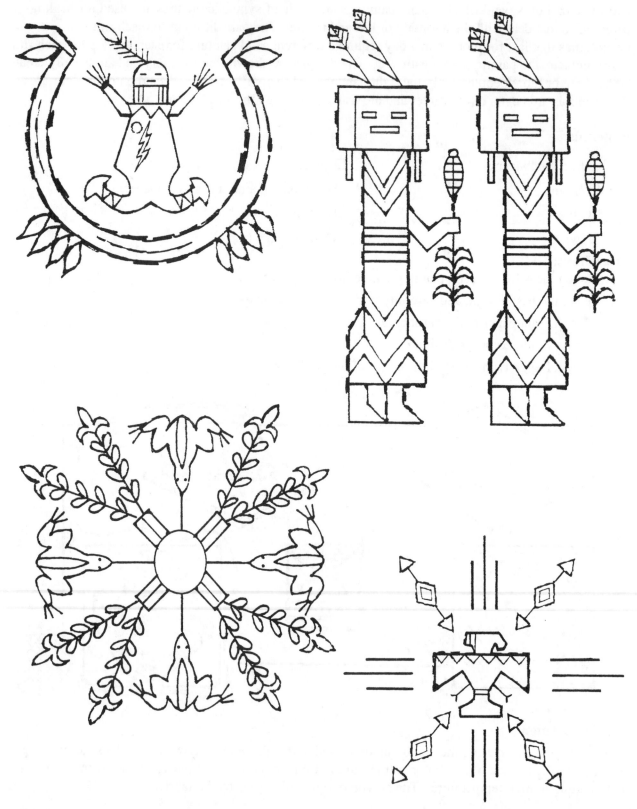

18

Crow Owner Sticks

Owner sticks were used by the Crow of Montana to designate their belongings. They were used to mark the position of an animal that had been hunted or food that had been gathered. Sometimes the sticks were used to measure distances, and sometimes they were used in games. Owner sticks were usually two to three feet (60 to 90 cm) long and specially designed by each family. Attached to the sticks were feathers, leather, bone, carvings, fur, beads, fibers, dried seeds, or any other kind of material desired.

Materials:

- ❏ 2' (60 cm) strong twig or dowel
- ❏ shorter twigs or dowels
- ❏ twine or colorful yarns
- ❏ scissors
- ❏ glue
- ❏ various decorative items that can be attached to the stick

Procedures:

1. Tie a shorter twig or dowel to the longer stick at right angles to form crossbeams.

2. Wrap twine or yarn on sections of the stick. Tie or glue in place.

3. Attach the decorative items to various locations on the stick.

Plains Indian Shield

The Native American Indians of the Great Plains created elaborate shields used primarily for protection. The large shields were made from animal hides stretched across bone or tree branches that had been softened and curved. They were usually decorated with strong, powerful symbols from nature. Popular symbols were buffalo, lightning, bear, antelope, and deer. Various lines and designs were also added. In some tribes, the shields were designed with four or six symbols. Four represented north, south, east, and west, and six symbolized the earth and sky.

Materials:

- ❏ white paper plate (dinner-sized)
- ❏ glue
- ❏ scissors
- ❏ pattern (page 21)
- ❏ crayons,
- ❏ 9" x 3" (23 cm x 8 cm) newsprint paper
- ❏ stapler
- ❏ watercolor paint and marking pens (optional)

Procedures to Make Shield:

1. On the back of a paper plate, draw Indian symbols or symbols of your own. Add other lines and designs if desired.

2. Color the designs with crayons. (Optional: paint over the entire plate with brown watercolor *after* the symbols have been colored.)

Procedures to Make Feathers:

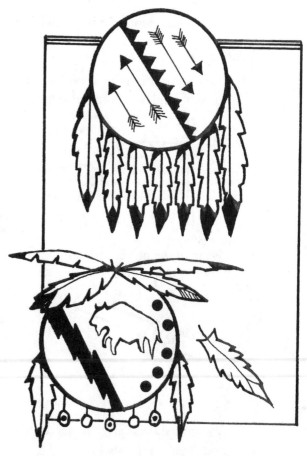

1. To make a feather, fold the newsprint paper in half. Using brown, white, and black crayons, draw diagonal lines on each half of the paper. Make the diagonals go up to the right on the right side, and up to the left on the left side.

2. Fold the paper in the reverse, and trace the feather pattern against the fold. (**Note:** if the diagonals on the other side are going up, then trace the pattern pointing up as well.) Cut out the feather, leaving the fold intact. Cut thin, diagonal slashes toward the fold, as shown on the pattern.

3. Open the fold, and gently squeeze and crush the feather to give it dimension. Glue or staple the feather to the shield. Add more feathers, if desired.

Variations:

1. *Color:* Paint the plate using watercolor or tempera paint. After the plate has dried, use black marking pens to create the designs on the shields.

2. *Brown Bags:* Instead of using paper plates, tear a large, circular shape from a grocery bag to use as the animal hide for the shield. Water-softened kite sticks can be shaped and dried in a circle to create the frame. Use brown yarn to "sew" the paper to the frame. Decorate as desired.

Plains Indian Shield:
Feather Pattern

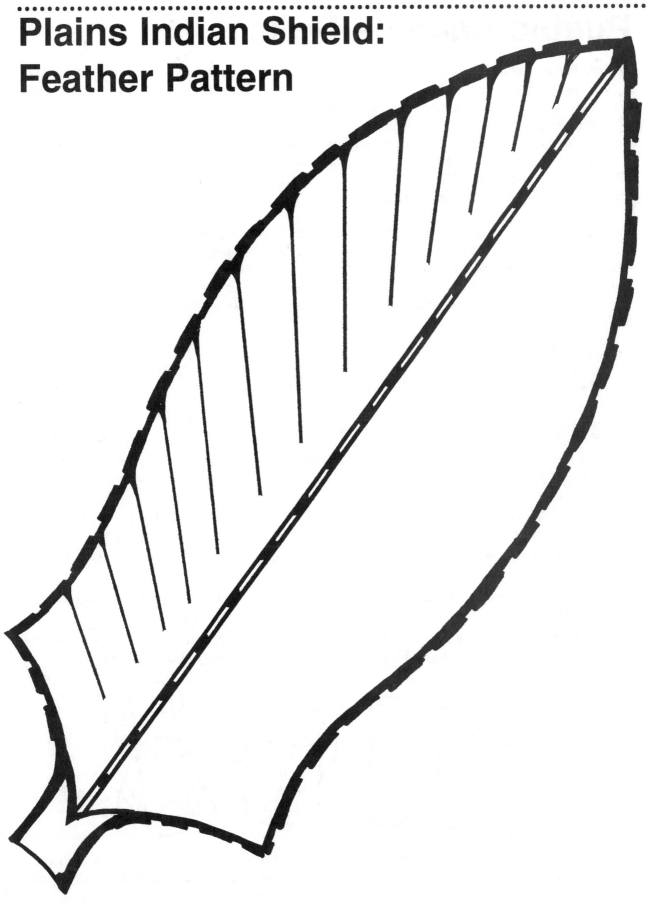

Pueblo Kachina Dolls

*I*n the Pueblo culture, the Kachina are divine spirits who act as intermediaries between man and god. The Kachina are never worshiped, but are thought of as benevolent spirits and friends. They are named according to what they represent, usually animals, crops, or human attributes.

Kachinas live with the tribe for the first six months of the year. They allow themselves to be seen only if the men perform traditional rituals and dances while wearing symbolic Kachina masks. The dances often depict sacred myths and legends. The spirit of the Kachina then become present by temporarily transforming the performer wearing the mask.

The men of the village carve and decorate small wooden dolls representing some of the 300 different types of Kachinas. These are given to children to teach them the identities of the Kachinas by recognizing particular symbols, colors, and costuming. Each tribe has its own special versions and styles of Kachinas. The masks on the Kachinas do not show human features in a realistic style. The masks are covered with special colors or symbols that represent the important things in life: rain, sunlight, fertility, and crops.

Materials:

- ❑ 4 colors of 9" x 12" (23 cm x 30 cm) construction paper
- ❑ scissors
- ❑ glue
- ❑ pencil
- ❑ ruler
- ❑ design page (p. 23)
- ❑ fine-point black marking pen (optional)
- ❑ feathers (optional)

Procedures:

1. Roll and glue the paper for the body into a 9" (23 cm) long tube. Set aside to dry.
2. Select another sheet of paper for the mask, and fold a lengthwise strip 3" (8 cm) wide. Cut on the fold.
3. Glue the 3" (8 cm) strip on top of one end of the body tube. Match the seam of the strip on top of the seam of the body tube. The seams are the back side of the Kachina.
4. Finish the Kachina using cutout paper to create the shapes and designs on page 23. Use marking pens to draw additional designs, if desired. Staple or glue feathers to the headdress.

Headdress Variation:

Create a Kachina headdress using 12" x 18" (30 cm x 45 cm) sheets of construction paper. Roll and glue the paper to make a 12" (30 cm) tall tube. Cut up smaller sheets of paper to make the decorative shapes.

Pueblo Kachina Dolls:
Sample Designs

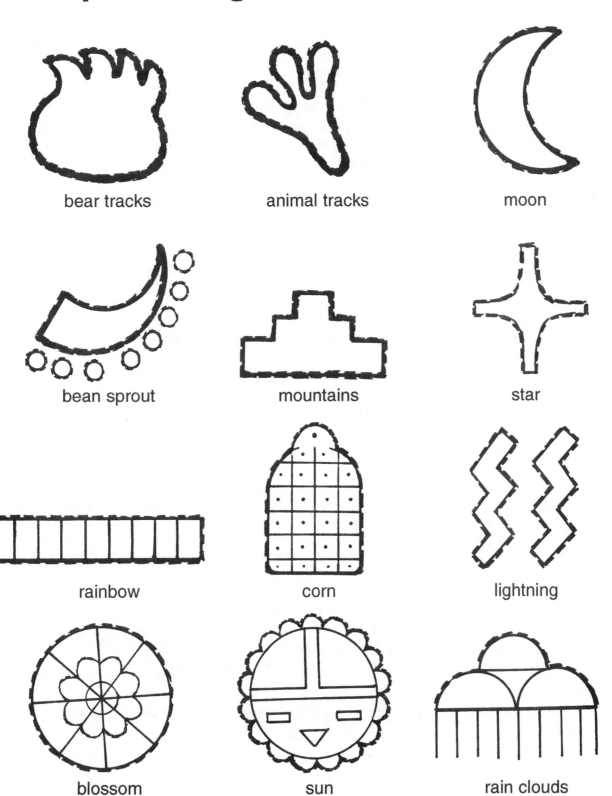

bear tracks

animal tracks

moon

bean sprout

mountains

star

rainbow

corn

lightning

blossom

sun

rain clouds

Three-Dimensional Pueblo Architecture

/n 1540, the Spanish explorer, Coronado, traveled northward out of Mexico and crossed the Rio Grande River into the southwest region of North America. He came across people who had developed well organized towns and villages. Coronado called the settlements of this region *pueblos,* the Spanish word for towns. This term is used to identify both the towns and the people who lived in them.

The culture of the Indians of the Southwest remained primarily in Arizona, New Mexico, and the southern parts of Utah and Colorado. The Hopi are among the most notable of the Pueblo Indians. The hills in the Southwest, mesas, have flat tops and steep, rocky sides. Pueblo structures were built on the mesas. Earlier Southwest Indians built their villages into the sides of cliffs.

The Pueblos lived in compact structures made of adobe clay shaped into oblong lumps. The buildings have flat roofs and rectangular walls often several stories high. For defensive purposes, the exterior entry doors were not built on the ground floor. Ladders led up to upper levels and could be pulled up in times of trouble. The structures of the Pueblo Indians were built around a central village area. In the middle of this area were *kivas,* ceremonial rooms that were built partly or entirely underground. Murals depicting sacred subjects were often painted on the adobe walls.

Materials: 2 half-gallon (2 liter) milk cartons, ruler, glue, scissors, fine-grained sand, paintbrush, light brown tempera paint, paint mixing bowl, waxed paper, 9" x 12" (23 cm x 30 cm), corrugated cardboard, 8 pieces of wood dowel cut into ½" (1.25 cm) segments, greenery (optional), clay (optional), brown thread

Procedures:

1. Cut off the top of each of the milk cartons. Cut one carton 2" (5 cm) shorter than the other. Clean and dry the insides of the cartons.

2. Turn the cartons so that the flat bottom is now the roof. Cut one rectangular door on each carton near the roof.

3. Glue the cartons together as illustrated.

4. Mix the tempera paint together with the sand and glue. Place the glued cartons on a sheet of waxed paper; carefully paint the structure with the glue/sand mixture. Let it dry overnight.

5. Glue the pueblo structure onto the cardboard.

6. Cut the twigs into desired lengths to make a ladder. Glue the twigs together, then wrap the joints with thread as illustrated. Glue the ladder in place by a doorway.

7. Glue the wood dowels along the top edge of a few of the pueblo walls to represent woods poles used for roof support.

8. **Optional:** Decorate the exterior of the pueblo as desired with tiny clay bowls and greenery.

Northwest Indian Symbols

*T*he Indians of the Northwest lived in a narrow region of land from the Yakutat Bay in Alaska south through British Columbia and down to the northern end of California. When the first explorers reached this area, they found an advanced culture based primarily on the riches of the sea and the forests. The explorers referred to them by the languages they spoke. The most prominent of these were the Tlingit in Alaska, the Haida and Kwakiutl in British Columbia, the Nootka, Salish, and Chinook in the area of Washington, and Karok and Yurok in the area of northern California.

In the Northwest, social order and religion were intertwined. The villages were each independent units organized around a clan of related families. The clans were named after creatures from nature that the Indians believed held a special relationship with humans. Common clan names were Raven, Eagle, Wolf, Otter, Whale, and Bear. Images of these supernatural creatures were incorporated into aspects of daily life.

Village craftsmen would decorate every inch of an object with symmetrical symbols and shapes that depicted specific clan animals. Usually the head was shown as two profiles touching each other. The rest of the body was divided in the center. Often the head would be the only recognizable part of the animal. The body area would be intricately filled with various related shapes. Examples of the art forms can be found on all types of objects and possessions. The most famous are ceremonial masks, totem poles, woven blankets, cedar boxes, utensils, and weapons. Designs from the Northwest Indians are considered by many to be the finest and most elaborate of the Indians of North America.

Materials:

- ❑ 12" x 18" (30 cm x 45 cm) manilla drawing paper
- ❑ pencil
- ❑ wide paintbrush
- ❑ paint mixing bowl
- ❑ diluted turquoise tempera paint
- ❑ crayons (black, red, and white)
- ❑ newspaper to cover painting area
- ❑ sample designs page (p. 26)

Procedures:

1. Design a clan animal on the paper. (You can use the sample design page to get ideas.) The shapes should be large to fill up the entire paper. Draw lightly with the pencil.

2. Color the design with a *heavy* application of crayon. Outline some areas, and leave the inside of those shapes empty of color.

3. Carefully dilute tempera paint with water in the mixing bowl. Experiment on a scrap piece of crayoned paper to create a consistency of paint that will not cover the crayon areas. This process is called *crayon resist*.

4. Use the wide paintbrush to cover the entire paper with turquoise. Brush strokes should all go in the same direction. The paint should cling only to the areas *without* crayon wax. Some paint residue may remain on top of the crayon areas. **Note:** If the paint conceals the crayon areas, use crumpled paper towels to blot the excess water. When the paper is dry, it will give the design a "weathered" look.

Northwest Indian Symbols:
Sample Designs

26   © 1994 Teacher Created Materials, Inc.

Northwest Indian Totem Poles

*T*he best known artifacts of the Northwest Indians are their totem poles. The Haida attached a totem pole to the front of their log houses, and cut an entry door into the pole. Other carved and painted poles were used as beams within the building's structure. Clan crests were carved around the sides of the poles, along with symbols representing a legend or an event in clan history. Often a totem pole was erected in the memory of a dead chief, and important events honoring the life of the chief were recorded on it. The grave of a chief was marked by a such a pole, and sometimes the body was placed inside. The animals representing the spirit of the clan or village were usually carved on top of the pole.

Materials:

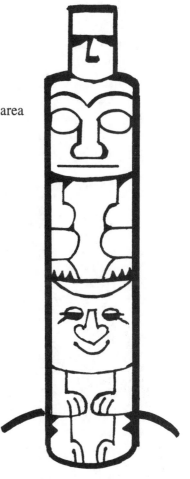

- ❏ several tin cans all the same size
- ❏ masking tape
- ❏ brown grocery bags
- ❏ bowl
- ❏ construction paper
- ❏ wide, black marking pen
- ❏ glue
- ❏ liquid starch
- ❏ cardboard
- ❏ scissors
- ❏ large stones
- ❏ newspaper to cover work area

Procedures:

1. Stuff a crumpled paper bag into one tin can. Place the stones on top. This will help keep the totem pole from falling over when it is finished.

2. Glue the remaining cans on top of each other, and then wrap the joints with masking tape.

3. Cut out beak and wing shapes from the cardboard. Glue or securely tape in place.

4. Tear a paper bag into short strips. Dip the strips in the starch, and then cover the entire totem pole with the strips, overlapping them in a vertical direction. Apply an extra layer of strips for greater strength.

5. While the totem pole is drying, draw and cut out decorative shapes from construction paper. The shapes should be symmetrical and resemble clan animals.

6. Glue the paper shapes to the surface of the totem pole. Outline with a wide, black marking pen.

Variations:

1. *Color:* Paint the designs on the totem pole using red, black, and blue tempera paint.

2. *Animal Topper:* Crumple tin foil into a three-dimensional animal shape. Glue or tape to the top of the totem pole. Cover with paper bag strips and decorate.

3. *Paper:* Use 12" x 18" (30 cm x 45 cm) brown construction paper for the totem pole. Roll lengthwise and glue to form an 18" (45 cm) tube. Decorate with other cut paper shapes in selected colors. Wings and beaks can be cut from brown paper and added.

Asian Art

*A*sian art stems from an old and valued tradition. Before written history, there is record of the beautiful porcelains, carvings, scroll paintings, and sculptures that have come to be identified with the richness of Asia's artistic culture.

Because the continent of Asia is comprised of many nations and cultures, the art of Asia is diverse as well. Yet in style and subject, it is usually distinct from western art. Religion is a key factor to much of Asia's art, and harmony is a vital concept to many of its religions. The art often reflects this.

Consider, for example, Buddhist and Islamic art. For both, spiritual life is key, but the tenets of each faith make the artistic expression somewhat different. Buddhist art often features Buddha. Animals, people, and nature are also featured, though the art itself usually makes clear man's small part in the balance of nature and the universe. The art of Islam, which makes itself seen in elaborate architecture (like the Taj Mahal), illustrations, ceramics, glassware, textiles, rugs, and more, features intricate patterns of leaves, stems, and so forth. According to Muslim law, no humans or animals are to be featured.

Activities

○ **Chinese Zodiac Calendar**

○ **Chinese Dragon**

○ **Chinese Moon Festival Lantern**

○ **Southeast-Asian Theater Headdress**

○ **Japanese Daruma Dolls**

○ **Japanese Fish Rubbing**

○ **Japanese Fish Kites**

Chinese Zodiac Calendar

*C*hinese astrology is based upon a cycle of twelve years instead of twelve months. A person's attributes may be told from the animals represented in the zodiac symbols. Many versions of the astrology legend are told among the Chinese people.

God called all the animals of the world to come see him. He promised gifts to those that came. The first to arrive was the rat, followed by the ox, tiger, and rabbit. Then came the dragon, snake, horse, and sheep. The boar was the last animal to arrive. God gave to these animals a special gift. He allowed them to control certain years and project their characteristics to them. Each year was then represented by an animal. Because the rat arrived first, the cycle started with the Year of the Rat.

- **The Rat:** symbol of industry and prosperity, associated with the god of wealth. (1972, 1984, 1996)

- **The Ox:** symbol of spring and agriculture. (1973, 1985, 1997)

- **The Tiger:** symbol of courage, dignity, and sternness. (1974, 1986, 1998)

- **The Rabbit:** symbol of long life, associated with the moon. (1975, 1987, 1999)

- **The Dragon:** symbol of goodness, associated with water, rain, rivers, and the oceans. (1976, 1988, 2000)

- **The Snake:** symbol of flattery and cunning, believed to have supernatural powers. (1977, 1989, 2001)

- **The Horse:** symbolizes speed, perseverance, and travel. (1978, 1990, 2002)

- **The Sheep:** symbol of a retired, slow-paced life. (1979, 1991, 2003)

- **The Monkey:** controls both good and evil spirits, regarded as a messenger and protector of roadways. (1980, 1992, 2004)

- **The Rooster:** associated with five virtues—courage, benevolence, faithfulness, the literary spirit, and the warrior spirit. (1981, 1993, 2005)

- **The Dog:** symbol for a guardian and good luck in the future. (1970, 1982, 1994)

- **The Boar:** symbol of the wealth of the forests, but poverty to people if found in the home. (1971, 1983, 1995)

Materials:

- ❑ clay
- ❑ plastic knife
- ❑ water bowl
- ❑ newspaper to cover work area
- ❑ diluted red or black tempera paint in a large bucket

- ❑ rolling pin
- ❑ toothpick
- ❑ dinner-sized paper plate
- ❑ calendar design page (page 31)
- ❑ kiln (if firing is desired)

Chinese Zodiac Calendar *(cont.)*

Procedures:

1. Flatten a clay slab with the rolling pin until it reaches a diameter slightly larger than the paper plate, and about ½" (1.25 cm) thick.

2. Place the paper plate on top of the clay, and trace the circle shape with a plastic knife. Remove the plate and smooth the edges carefully with a small amount of water.

3. Poke a hole, about the diameter of a pencil, near the edge of the clay circle.

4. Use a toothpick to draw lines lightly on the clay, dividing the circle into twelve sections. (A template may be used.)

5. In each section, draw the Chinese character for each animal of the zodiac with a toothpick. (See page 31.) Begin with the rat at the top by the hole.

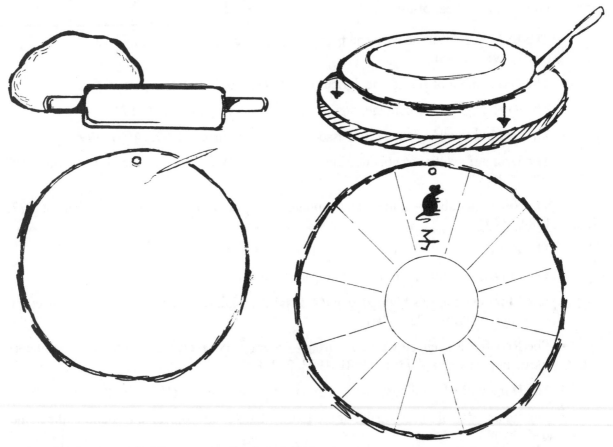

6. After the clay has dried for a week, fire it in a kiln.

7. Dunk the fired clay into the bucket of tempera paint to create a stained effect on the clay. The paint will also darken the incised lines of the Chinese characters.

8. Tie yarn or ribbon through the hole for hanging.

Variations:

1. *Animal Pictures:* Students may wish to draw animals on the clay or write in the English translations for the animals and the years.

2. *Paper:* Create the entire project from construction paper and poster board.

Chinese Zodiac Calendar:
Sample Design

Chinese Dragon

*T*he Chinese dragon is a symbol of strength and goodness. It is the emblem of Chinese emperors, and it is the most sacred animal. The dragon appears once a year, during the Chinese New Year, to wish everyone good luck, wealth, and peace.

The most anticipated character in the Chinese New Year Parade is the Dancing Dragon. An enormous head is usually made from papier-mâché, and it is carried by hand or on a pole by a specially selected performer. The rest of the body is so long that it requires many more dancers to carry it. The dragon dances and twists along the parade route, often blowing smoke from the nostrils. It is usually decorated with red and orange colors, which symbolize joy. The head is decorated with paint, glitter, tassels, and dangling ornaments. The body is made from painted silk or colorful fabric streamers.

Materials:

- ❑ school-sized milk carton (clean and dry)
- ❑ scissors
- ❑ glue
- ❑ bendable plastic drinking straw
- ❑ pencil
- ❑ glitter
- ❑ 9" x 12" (23 cm x 30 cm) red, black, and white construction paper
- ❑ crayons
- ❑ thin tissue paper streamers of various colors and lengths
- ❑ patterns (page 33)
- ❑ sample design (page 34)

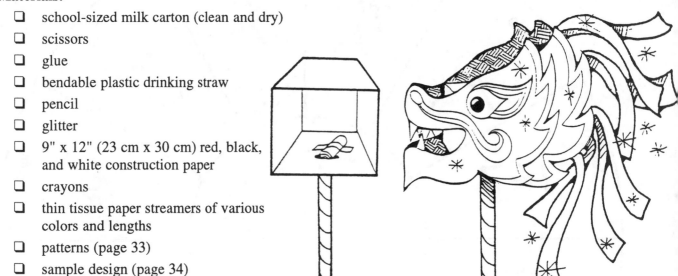

Procedures:

1. Cut off the top of the milk carton.
2. Cover the exterior of the carton with red paper.
3. Turn the bottom side of the carton to become the front of the dragon's face. The open side will be the back of the head.
4. Poke a hole into the center of what is now the bottom side of the carton. Insert a bendable plastic straw and tape in position as shown.
5. Draw the pattern shapes on the construction paper and then cut out. Use colors as desired. *Cut the head on a fold.*
6. Glue all facial features to each side of the head. Add designs with a black marking pen or crayon.
7. Glue the outer head spikes to the edges of the box on two sides.
8. Glue the head piece to the box. The dragon's snout will extend out from the box.
9. Add glitter where desired.
10. Glue several streamers around the open side of the carton (the back of the head).

Chinese Dragon: Patterns

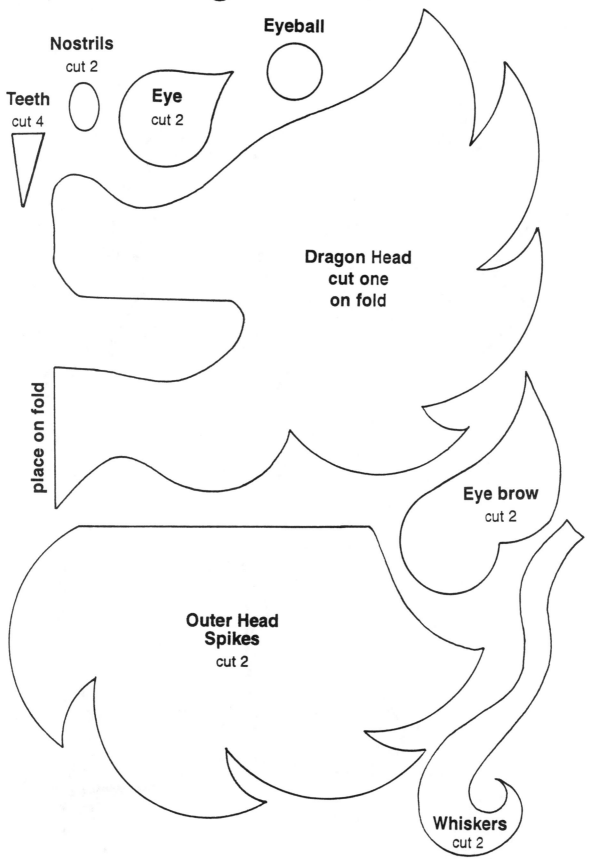

Eyeball

Nostrils
cut 2

Teeth
cut 4

Eye
cut 2

**Dragon Head
cut one
on fold**

place on fold

Eye brow
cut 2

**Outer Head
Spikes**

cut 2

Whiskers
cut 2

Chinese Dragon: Sample Design

Chinese Moon Festival Lantern

*T*he Moon Festival is celebrated on the fifteenth day of the eight month of the lunar calendar, usually October. To celebrate a good harvest, families gather to create beautiful lanterns, eat traditional foods, and participate in a community-wide lantern parade. The lantern symbolizes the glow of the harvest moon.

Materials:

- ❏ 4 sheets of red construction paper 4½" x 6" (11.5 cm x 15 cm)
- ❏ 4 sheets of white paper 3" x 4½" (7.5 cm x 11.5 cm)
- ❏ scissors
- ❏ single-hole paper punch
- ❏ gold glitter
- ❏ glue
- ❏ stapler,
- ❏ 4 paper "beads"
- ❏ red or black crayon or marking pen
- ❏ thick black or red yarn
- ❏ sample writing page (page 36)

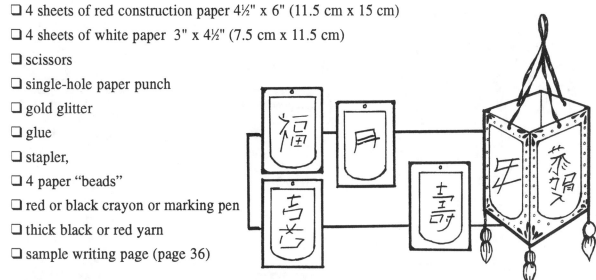

Procedures:

1. On each sheet of white paper, draw a Chinese word in a vertical direction with crayon or pen. (See page 36.) Print the English translation toward the bottom of the white rectangle, if desired. Optional: cut a curved shape or fancy edge to one of the short sides of each red rectangle. (See illustration.)
2. Glue each white rectangle to the center of each red sheet of construction paper.
3. Draw a border pattern around the edges of the construction paper. Apply glitter as desired.
4. Staple each red rectangle together as illustrated.
5. Punch a hole in the top center of each rectangle. Attach yarn to hang the lantern.
6. Make two yarn tassels and paper beads. Attach at opposite sides of the lantern. Glue or staple in place.

Chinese Moon Festival Lantern: Sample Writing

Rain

Moon

Happy

New

Year

Long Life

Good Luck

Happiness

Wealth

36

Southeast-Asian Theater Headdress

*D*ance and drama troupes were part of the royal courts of Cambodia, Thailand, and Burma from the ninth through fifteenth centuries. The most popular were masked dance-mimes who used elaborate headdresses as part of their costumes. These dance-plays were known as *lakon-kawl*. Headdresses and costumes were adorned with sequins, jewels, or peacock feathers, and they were made from beautifully embellished fabrics. Ornate designs of circles, spirals, and curved lines decorated the surface. Early theater did not use elaborate scenery, thereby making the costumes, headdresses, and crowns very important to the production. The western musical production, *The King and I*, showcases many elaborate versions of these headdresses.

Materials:

- ❑ 12" x 18" (30 cm x 45 cm) poster board
- ❑ 12" x 18" (30 cm x 45 cm) paper
- ❑ heavy cord
- ❑ scissors
- ❑ pencil
- ❑ glue
- ❑ aluminum foil
- ❑ gold acrylic paint
- ❑ small sponge
- ❑ decorating material such as sequins, beads, feathers, buttons, etc.

Procedures:

1. Fold the paper in half, matching the 12" (30 cm) edges.
2. Draw half of a headdress shape on the paper along the fold to create your own headdress design (or use the pattern provided on page 38).
3. Cut out the pattern. Unfold and place it on top of the poster board. Trace around the pattern, and then cut it out.
4. Draw spirals, circles, coils, and curved lines for decoration.
5. Glue lengths of cord or heavy yarn on top of the pencil designs.
6. Spread glue over some areas of the cardboard. Glue a length of tinfoil on top of the cardboard to cover the headdress. Begin in the center and *carefully* press the foil around the curved shapes.
7. Glue aluminum foil-covered poster board shapes to empty areas of the headdress.
8. Sponge gold acrylic paint on the foil to highlight the raised surfaces.
9. Decorate with desired materials and aluminum foil streamers.
10. Staple a 2" (5 cm) wide band to the backside if the headdress is to be worn.

Southeast-Asian Theater
Headdress: Pattern

Place this edge on fold.

38

Japanese Daruma Dolls

*T*he Japanese daruma doll symbolizes the spirit of courage and determination. No matter how many times you push this roly-poly doll, it always returns to an upright position.

The doll, which has no arms, legs, or eyes, is usually given to someone who is starting a new business. If the business is successful, the owner gathers with friends a year later to paint in the eyes of the doll. The daruma doll is also a traditional part of New Year celebrations. Each year, a new daruma doll is purchased by the family as a symbol of good luck. At the end of the year, the old doll is burned during a joyful celebration, and the new doll is welcomed into the home.

The dolls are created from various materials and often covered with gold-embroidered red fabrics.

Materials:

- ❑ plastic egg
- ❑ stone (to act as a weight inside the egg)
- ❑ hot glue gun
- ❑ cardboard circle with the same diameter measurement as the plastic egg
- ❑ starch
- ❑ paper towels
- ❑ bowl
- ❑ pencil, paint
- ❑ thin, black yarn
- ❑ glue
- ❑ gold glitter

Procedures:

1. Open the plastic egg and glue the stone into the bottom half.

2. Glue the egg closed.

3. Glue the cardboard circle to the bottom of the egg.

4. Place short strips of masking tape from the cardboard circle up the sides of the egg, as illustrated.

5. Cover the entire egg structure with short pieces of paper towels dipped in starch (papier-mâché). Make sure the layers of paper towel overlap.

6. After the structure dries, paint on the face and decorate the doll with tiny, painted flowers. Be sure to paint closed eyes or empty circles where the eyes should be.

7. Attach thin black yarn for hair.

Japanese Fish Rubbing

*T*he ancient art of *gyo-taku* evolved from an even older Chinese tradition of stone rubbing. This was a method of copying inscriptions that were carved into stone. The Japanese borrowed this print-making technique, and developed it into the regional folkcraft of fish rubbing. In coastal fishing villages of Japan and other areas abundant with fish, this art form is still created.

Materials:
- ❑ whole fish (not gutted or scaled)
- ❑ heavy white tissue paper
- ❑ black ink (block printing ink or tempera may be substituted for the black ink)
- ❑ small paint roller or brayer or large, wide paintbrush
- ❑ paper towels
- ❑ newspaper to cover the work area
- ❑ watercolors or crayons
- ❑ paper towels

Procedures:

1. Cover the work area with layers of newspaper. Place the fish on top of the newspaper. Pat the fish dry with paper towels.

2. Position the fish and spread the fins where necessary. Place small wads of paper towels under the fins to raise them.

3. Roll ink lightly over the fish.

4. Lay a sheet of tissue paper over the fish and gently rub with your hands on the surface of the paper.

5. Slowly peel away the paper to reveal the print of the fish.

6. Pat the fish dry, and repeat the procedures to create more prints.

7. When the prints have dried, lightly color some areas of the fish with watercolors or crayons.

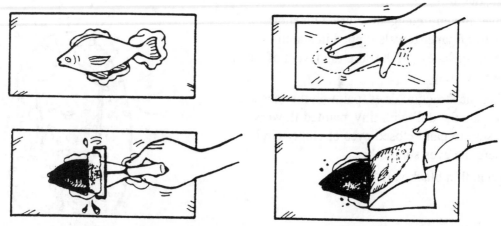

Japanese Fish Kites

*B*oys' Day is a holiday celebrated in Japan on May 5th. Traditionally, male children of the family create kites in the shape of fish, called *kol nobori*. The eldest boy makes the largest kite, and the youngest boy makes the smallest. These colorful kites are patterned after large carp, symbolizing courage and determination, qualities the boys hope to achieve.

Materials:

❏ colored tissue paper 18" x 24" (45 cm x 60 cm)

❏ white paper strip 12" x 1" (30 cm x 2.5 cm)

❏ colored tissue paper 12" x 9" (30 cm x 22.5 cm)

❏ yarn

❏ glue

❏ single-hole paper punch

❏ scissors

❏ patterns (pages 42-43)

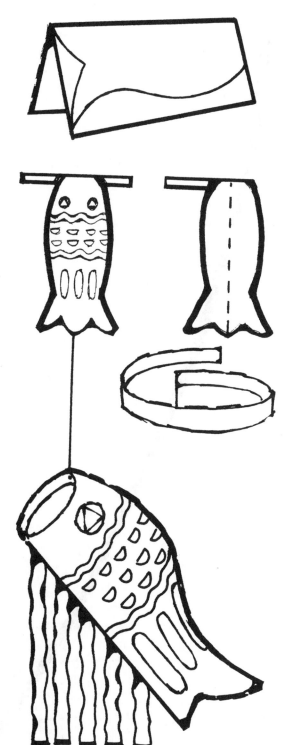

Procedures:

1. Fold the large sheet of tissue paper in half lengthwise.

2. Attach the two halves of the fish pattern together. Draw the fish shape against the fold of the paper, using the pattern.

3. Carefully cut out the fish.

4. Open the folded shape, and glue the paper strip along the top straight edge of the fish. This will be used to form the mouth opening.

5. Turn over the fish and decorate with contrasting colors and fanciful shapes. Designs should be symmetrical and well balanced. Streamers and fins can be added.

6. When finished, turn the fish over to the wrong side. Apply dots of glue to the curved sides of the fish shape and glue together.

7. Cut off one end of the paper strip evenly with the head. Curve the strip into a circle, and glue to the inside of the head as shown in the illustration.

8. Punch a hole into the paper strip and attach yarn to hang the fish kite.

Suggestions:

1. Students can design a fish pattern of their own.

2. Use glue sparingly on tissue paper.

41   *TCM #617 MULTICULTURAL ART ACTIVITIES*

Japanese Fish Kites: Pattern (Top)

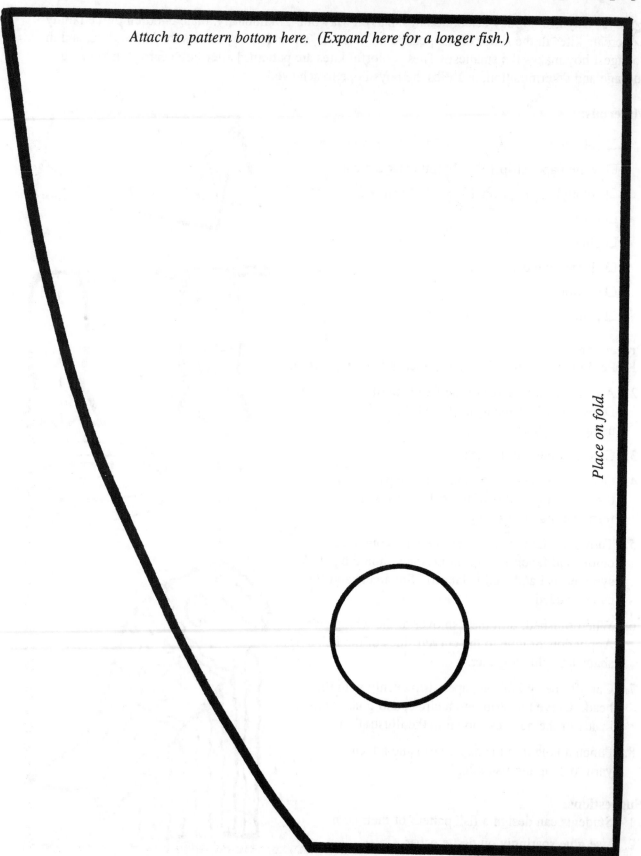

Attach to pattern bottom here. (Expand here for a longer fish.)

Place on fold.

Japanese Fish Kites:
Pattern (Bottom)

Place on fold.

Attach to pattern top here.

Hispanic Art

There is no central area that comprises Hispanic tradition. Instead, it is an amalgamation of cultures which share one factor in common: the Spanish language. The cultures also generally have in common Roman Catholic heritage.

If something is called "Hispanic," it may come from Mexico, Puerto Rico, Cuba, Spain, or any number of other countries in Central and South America. No one thing can be said to be true of all of these cultures in terms of their artistic expression. However, there does seem to be a feeling about Hispanic art which is like no other. It often contains a passion, or feeling of energy, which emanates from the work. Even religious subjects are seen in human frameworks, and the mood is powerful. To achieve this, Hispanic art is commonly vibrant, colorful, bold, and open. It does not apologize for its flavor, but rather embraces it. The art is like a song, rich in melody and diverse in sound.

Activities

○ **Simulated Mexican Tinware**

○ **Mexican Tree of Life**

○ **Huichol Ojo de Dios Weaving**

○ **Huichol Nierikas**

○ **Mexican Fiesta Doll**

○ **Mexican Bird Rattle**

○ **Spanish/Mexican Piñata**

Simulated Mexican Tinware

*T*he artistry of Mexican metalsmiths has been prized for centuries. Metalsmiths were men of importance and position in Aztec society. Gold and silver were mined and then crafted into unique, jewel-encrusted objects. The Spaniards who conquered Mexico at first valued the intricate artistry depicted in the metal; however, they eventually melted down the pieces into more functional shapes.

Skilled craftsmen from all over Europe came to Mexico to learn the varied techniques. But the Indians who taught them were not allowed to possess any of the precious metals for themselves. Fortunes were made by the Spaniards as Mexico became the most important silver-producing country in the New World, but of all the metals worked in Mexico, tin became the most popular because it was tin to which the people had access. Also, the metal is thin and flexible, easy to form into various shapes. The tinsmiths would then paint designs onto the surface, using the decorated tin to embellish frames, mirrors, candle holders, and ornaments.

Materials:

- ❑ cardboard
- ❑ scissors
- ❑ marking pens
- ❑ thread/yarn
- ❑ glue

- ❑ aluminum foil
- ❑ pencil
- ❑ tempera paint
- ❑ patterns (pages 46-47)

Procedures:

1. Draw a large animal or flower shape on the cardboard from the pattern provided.
2. Carefully cut out the shape.
3. Glue the aluminum foil (dull side out) to both sides of the cardboard.
4. Use marking pens or paint to decorate the shape with strong, vibrant lines.
5. Attach a thread or yarn for hanging the ornament.

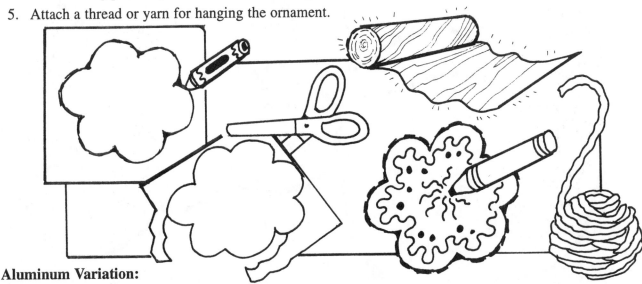

Aluminum Variation:

Aluminum sheets can be purchased from hardware stores and used as a substitute for tin. This material can be decorated with acrylic paints.

Simulated Mexican Tinware:
Patterns

Cut 2 wings.

Glue. Fold.

46

Simulated Mexican Tinware: Patterns *(cont.)*

Fold.

Fold.

Mexican Tree of Life

*T*he Tree of Life is an elaborate, candle-bearing sculpture, usually created out of clay. Because it is meant to depict the creation of nature, the tree is decorated with flowers, birds, animals, people, and fruit. Each Tree of Life is different, varying by height, size, intricacies, and number of candleholders (anywhere from one to perhaps a dozen).

The Tree of Life originated with the Moors and was brought to Spain in the eighth century. Eventually it was introduced into Mexico. The potters of Izucar de Matamoros in Puebla and the Metepec region of Mexico are famous for this elaborate artform.

Materials:

- ❑ short glass beverage bottle
- ❑ 3 tiny paper clips
- ❑ paper plate
- ❑ paintbrush
- ❑ self-hardening clay
- ❑ assorted clay tools
- ❑ tempera or acrylic paint

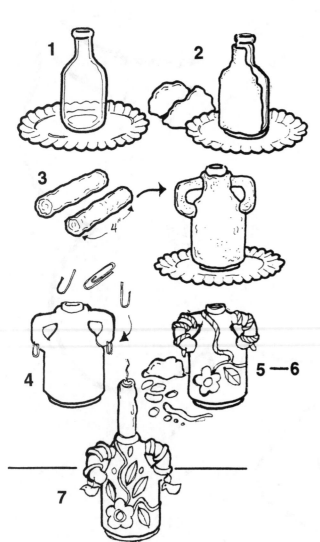

Procedures:

1. Place the bottle on top of the paper plate. The plate will help in rotating the sculpture and it will also serve as a work area.

2. Cover the bottle with the clay. Do not put clay on the bottom of the bottle or cover the top opening.

3. Roll out two pieces of clay to form fat, sausage shapes about 4" (10 cm) long. Attach these shapes as illustrated, one on each side of the bottle near the neck. These are the branches of the tree.

4. Break one paper clip in half to make two hooks. Insert the straight end into each branch. The curved hook end must be sticking out. This will be used to support hanging clay bird ornaments.

5. With the remaining clay, sculpt and attach large leaves and flower shapes to the tree. Make two birds and insert a paper clip into the top of each body.

6. When the clay sculpture hardens, paint it with vibrant colors. Hang the birds from the hooks on the branches.

7. Remove the Tree of Life from the paper plate. Insert a short candle into the neck of the bottle.

Huichol Ojo de Dios Weaving

*A*n ancient tradition of the Huichol of Jalisco, Mexico, Ojo de Dios (God's eye) weavings are good luck symbols believed to bring good fortune and health. The Huichol believe in the gods of nature. The crossed sticks that serve as the frame symbolize the four universal forces: earth, fire, water, and air. Colors have their special meaning, as well. Blue or turquoise represents the rain, green is fertility, yellow represents the sun, and brown is for the earth.

An Aztec legend tells of a beautiful princess who was born blind. The gods promised to restore her vision if anyone could duplicate the eye of God. One day, the sun's rays reflected a rainbow into the princess' tears. Using several yarns, her mother reproduced the colorful pattern. As soon as the weaving was complete, the princess regained her eyesight.

Materials:

- ❑ 2 sticks (twigs, dowels, tongue depressors, or ice cream sticks can also be used)
- ❑ several colors of yarn
- ❑ scissors

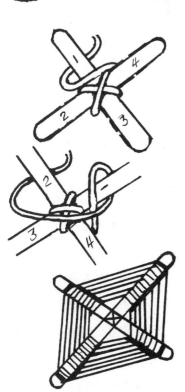

Procedures:

1. Select three colors of yarn and wind each into a small ball.
2. Choose the color to be placed in the center of the "eye." Use this ball of yarn to tie the sticks together firmly in the center. Turn to form right angles and tie securely.
3. Number the spokes counterclockwise from one to four. Spoke #1 must be at the top, spoke #2 to the left, and so on.
4. Hold the structure in the left hand at a point close to where the sticks intersect.
5. Holding the ball of yarn in the right hand, bring the yarn around spoke #1, going around from the back side. (See the illustration.)
6. Yarn will always wrap from the left side of the top spoke, travel around the back, and come out from the right side of the top spoke.
7. Rotate the sticks clockwise so that spoke #2 is now at the top and spoke #1 on the right.
8. Bring the yarn around spoke #3, going from the left side and around.
9. Rotate the sticks again clockwise so that spoke #3 is at the top and spoke #2 is on the right.
10. Continue the technique of rotation, wrapping until the desired width of the center eye is achieved. To change colors, cut the yarn ball and firmly tie the next color of yarn to the end. Proceed wrapping.

Huichol Nierikas

*T*he Huichol developed an artform using colorful yarns to create their pictures. Yarn painting is not an ancient craft but an adaptation from an old tradition. A *nierika* is a small wooden offering covered with yarn in designs representing requests to the gods. The Indians adapted this into a two-dimensional craft.

To make a nierikas, beeswax is coated onto the surface of a flat wooden board. A pointed stick is used to draw the design on the wax. Strands of yarn are then pressed into the wax to outline the shapes. More strands of yarn are pressed close together to fill in each shape and the entire background area.

The designs for the nierikas are a blend of fantasy and reality, using bright colors and swirling yarn patterns. Animals, snakes, corn, and the sun are popular images.

Materials:

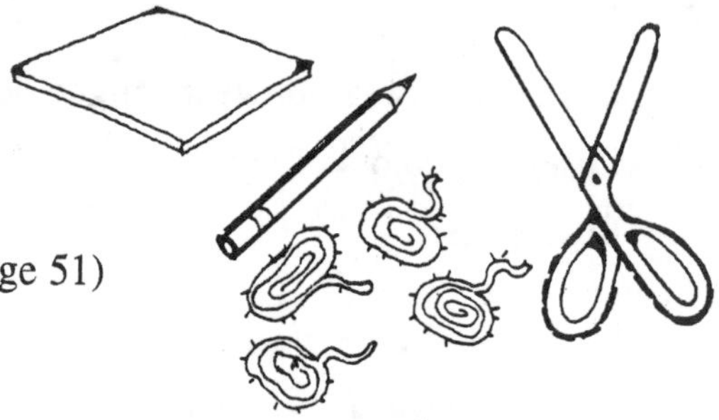

❏ 6" (15 cm) square piece of cardboard ❏ glue
❏ pencil ❏ scissors
❏ thin, colorful yarns ❏ patterns (page 51)

Procedures:

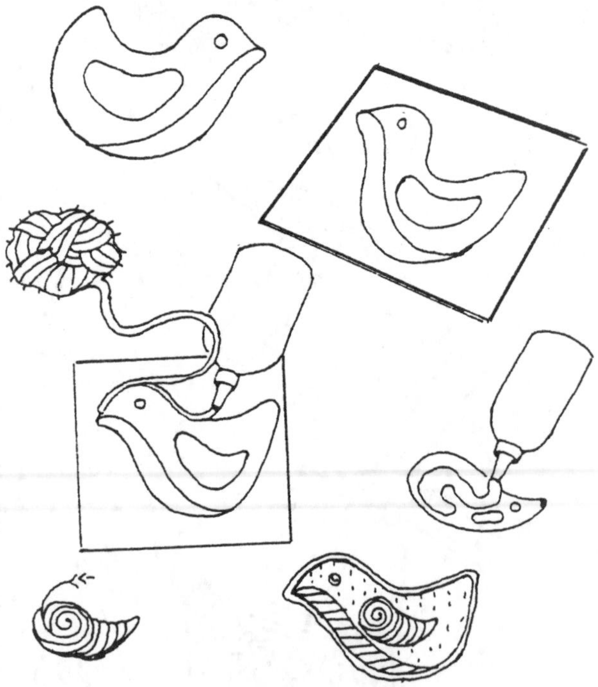

1. Draw a large shape in the center of the cardboard square.

2. Roll the desired yarn colors into small individual balls.

3. Select a yarn color to outline the shape. Apply glue to the pencil line and then press yarn on top of the glue. Cut off remaining yarn.

4. Select a second color of yarn. Apply glue to the center of the design and attach the end of the yarn as illustrated.

5. Fill in the center area with the yarn glued in a circular direction. The strands of yarn should be pressed close together.

6. Apply more glue to the area as needed. Continue to fill in the rest of the shape with yarn until the yarn meets the outlined edge.

7. After the center shape is completely filled in, begin to cover the background area with yarn, using the same technique but with a different color yarn.

8. To create a border around the picture, select another color of yarn and glue at least two rows around the edges.

Huichol Nierikas: Sample Designs

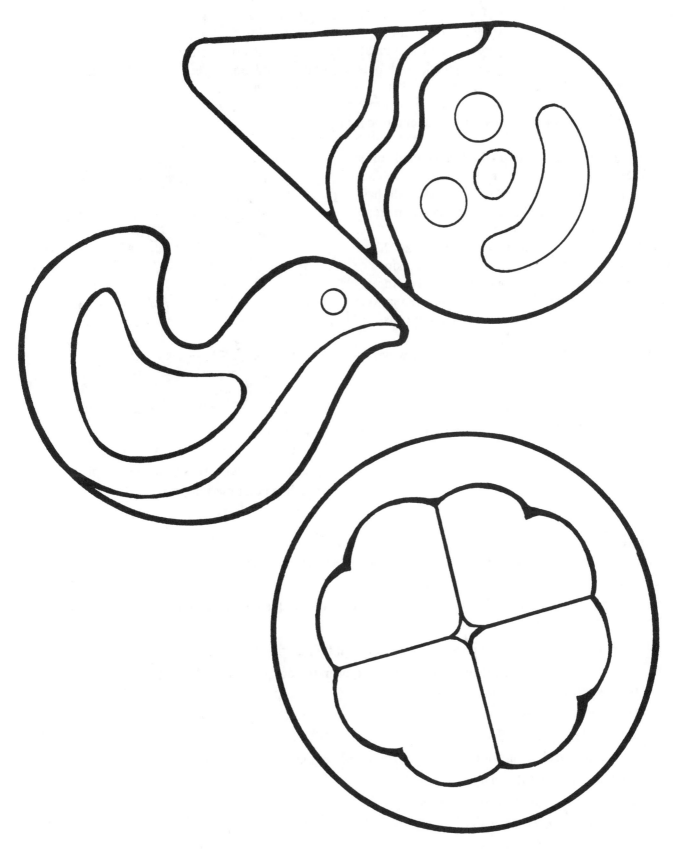

Mexican Fiesta Doll

The art of embroidery in Mexico is attributed to Xochiquetzal, the Aztec goddess of flowers and love. It is an ancient art, depicting both the place of origin and social hierarchy of the Indians who created and wore it. The Spanish, who had a great deal of ornamentation in their own fabrics and clothing, introduced new styles, methods, and tools for weaving and embroidery to the Mexicans. They also brought with them tassels, ribbons, and lace. Some of the designs and fabrics they brought had an oriental theme due to the Spanish trade in the Philippines. Yet despite European influences, each area of Mexico maintained its own traditional embroidery designs.

Geometric lines, stylized flowers, and animals often decorated clothing used for festive occasions. The fiesta, perhaps the most festive occasion of all, has always been an integral part of Mexican heritage. From Pre-Columbian Aztec rituals to the introduction of Christian themes by the Spanish, fiestas usually coincided with religious occasions. During these times of celebration, special clothing is worn. Men wear elaborately embroidered jackets with eagles or snakes crafted from gold threads. Female dancers wear magnificent dresses embroidered with colorful flowers on their wide, flowing skirts.

Materials:

- ❑ 9" x 12" (23 cm x 30 cm) white drawing paper
- ❑ scissors
- ❑ glue
- ❑ crayons
- ❑ glitter (optional)
- ❑ pencil
- ❑ tape
- ❑ tissue paper scraps (red, yellow, pink)
- ❑ fine point marking pens

Procedures:

1. Fit the pattern on the paper, trace with pencil, and cut out the pieces.
2. Draw designs on the dress where indicated.
3. Outline all the designs with the marking pens, and color in the designs with crayon.
4. Carefully draw the face and color it and the hair.
5. Tear small pieces of tissue paper and roll them tightly into tiny balls.
6. Glue the tissue paper balls in the hair, on a belt, or in the doll's hands to depict flowers. Glitter may be added, if desired.
7. Glue the doll together:
   a. Glue skirt flap A under side AA.
   b. Fold the head along the dotted line. Tape flap D at the neck on the back side.
   c. Glue shawl flap B under shawl side BB.
   d. Insert tab C into the back of the skirt.
   e. Glue arms under the shawl.

Mexican Fiesta Doll: Pattern

Mexican Bird Rattle

A popular tradition for New Year's celebrations and annual fiestas is the making of papier-mâché rattles. These joyful noisemakers are usually shaped to resemble colorful bird heads. The rattles are shaken to welcome generous spirits of the new year and to drive away any unhappy spirits remaining from the past.

Materials:

- ❏ 9" (23 cm) stick or dowel
- ❏ cardboard toilet paper tube
- ❏ scissors
- ❏ feathers
- ❏ starch
- ❏ bowls

- ❏ glue
- ❏ pencil
- ❏ masking tape
- ❏ used file folder
- ❏ paper towels
- ❏ beans or small stones

- ❏ newspaper to cover work area
- ❏ paintbrushes
- ❏ tempera or acrylic paint
- ❏ patterns (page 55)
- ❏ aluminum foil (optional)

Procedures:

1. Seal one end of the cardboard tube with masking tape.
2. Insert the stick into the open end and tape it in place.
3. Add beans into the tube and seal the end closed with tape.
4. Cut out a beak from the file folder and tape or glue it in place.
5. Tear short, narrow strips of paper towels. Dip them into the starch, and apply them on the rattle structure. Cover the entire rattle, except the handle, in this manner with two layers of paper towels.
6. Paint the rattle when it has dried thoroughly.
7. Glue features to the top of the head.

Variations:

1. *Round Heads:* To make a round head for the bird, crumple aluminum foil and tape it around the cardboard tube.
2. *Tissue Paper:* Instead of paint, cover the head with bright colors of tissue paper. Tear small pieces and apply by using a paintbrush dipped into acrylic polymer or diluted white glue.

Mexican Bird Rattle: Beak Patterns

Place dotted edge of each pattern on fold.

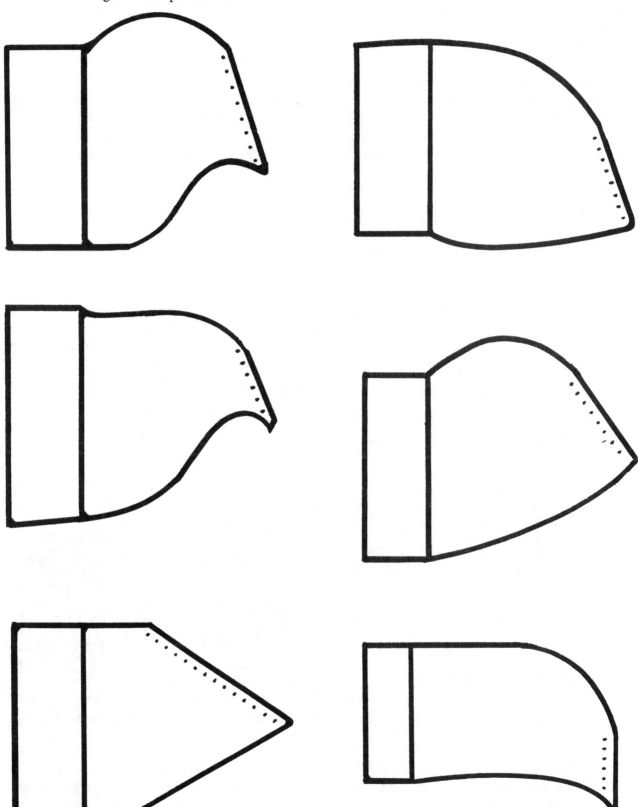

Spanish/Mexican Piñata

*T*he piñata is a large, colorfully decorated container made from cardboard and decorated with fancy paper. It is usually filled with candy, coins, and small toys. The piñata is hung over a tree branch with a rope. Blindfolded children take turns trying to break the piñata while it swings and spins. Adults join in the excitement by pulling on the rope while the children attempt to break open the piñata.

Originating in Italy during the Renaissance, the piñata was a festive party game. Guests filled a pottery piñata bowl with candy and nuts. The bowl was suspended by a rope, and the guests attempted to make the piñata swing wide to spill out the delicious contents. In Spain, the piñata was incorporated into Easter celebrations following Lent. Then, about 400 years ago, the piñata was brought to Mexico by Spanish explorers. It eventually became a traditional part of Christmas and birthday celebrations.

Materials:

- ❏ inflated balloon (tied closed)
- ❏ liquid starch
- ❏ 12" (30 cm) length of string
- ❏ paper towels
- ❏ bowls
- ❏ colorful tissue paper
- ❏ scissors
- ❏ newspaper to cover work area
- ❏ glue

Procedures:

1. Tie the yarn on the neck of the balloon and suspend it from a reachable work area.

2. Tear paper towels into short pieces. Dip each piece into the starch, then attach the moistened strip to the balloon. Cover the entire balloon with two or three layers of paper towels.

3. Let the piñata dry completely, about 4 days, and then cut a small hole close to the top.

4. Cut strips of tissue paper 18" x 5" (45 cm x 13 cm). Fold in half lengthwise.

5. Cut slits into the tissue along the folded edges of the paper.

6. Glue the folded edges apart from each other so they do not meet. This will make the cut slits puff up. (See illustration.)

7. Glue each length of ruffled tissue paper to cover the entire piñata. Leave the hole area open to insert small candy or other items.

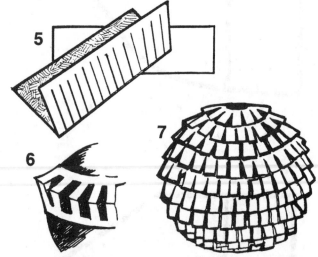

Variations:

1. *Simple Piñata:* Use a large cereal box instead of a balloon. Cover the entire box with the ruffled tissue paper, leaving the top open to insert treats. Poke two holes into the box and insert string to hang the piñata.

2. *Fancy Piñata:* To make a fancier piñata, attach three-dimensional cardboard pieces to create specific forms, such as a clown head, cake, animals, and so forth. Attach the cardboard pieces to the balloon or cereal box and decorate as desired.

Colonial American Art

*C*olonial art finds its home between two cornerstones: the elaborate and the practical. Highly skilled artisans often employed their craft in the production of functional objects needed by the hard-working people. Yet the class of rich elite (or those who wished to appear as such) also existed, and for them only the finest furnishings, architecture, silver, china, and portraiture would do. One might think of colonial art on one hand as stiff and stylized; on the other hand, it is folksy and familiar.

At first, the wealthy class commissioned portraits by the only available artists—those of little training. These were followed by professionals whose style was often elevated to a romantic and heroic vein. Yet in the homes of the masses, a more comfortable artistry was present. Quilts of great skill and intricacy could be seen in every dwelling, valued (and necessary) for both their warmth and their beauty. Stencilers, dollmakers, woodworkers, and silversmiths flourished. Craftsmen and women were necessary to the production of serviceable tools and equipment which required great skill in their production, such as in the arts of barrelmaking and smithing. Design and function fused into one, and a style was created that blossoms even today.

Activities

○ **Fraktur Design Birth Certificate**

○ **Sgraffito Plates**

○ **Bargello Needlepoint**

○ **Barn Hex Symbols**

○ **Corn Husk Dolls**

○ **Quilling**

○ **Quilting**

Fraktur Design Birth Certificate

*T*he English and German immigrants who settled in Pennsylvania brought with them an abundant source of folk decoration from their homelands. Soon these designs took on their own character, and they are recognized today as Pennsylvania Dutch Folk Art.

The word *fraktur* comes from the sixteenth century German type-style comprised of thin shapes, pointed ends, and bristling serifs. Among the Pennsylvania Germans, the term was used for ornamental drawings and calligraphy. The most popular designs were hearts, tulips, pomegranates, birds, unicorns, angels, and other fanciful creatures. These designs were usually drawn in a symmetrical layout.

In many fraktur designs, special documents, such as marriage and birth certificates, were scripted within a heart shape. Colorful flowers were drawn and painted around the heart. Sometimes urn or vase shapes were also used to contain the information.

Materials:

- ❏ 12" x 18" (30 cm x 45 cm) drawing paper
- ❏ pencils
- ❏ construction paper
- ❏ sample designs (pages 59-60)
- ❏ crayons
- ❏ diluted black tempera paint or black India ink
- ❏ paper towels

Procedures:
1. Carefully tear the edges of the drawing paper. This will give the birth certificate an antique look.
2. Draw a large heart in the center of the paper. Print the name and date of birth in the center of the heart.
3. Add other Pennsylvania Dutch designs around the heart. (See pages 59-60.) Color the designs with a heavy application of crayon.
4. Apply *thinned* black tempera paint over the surface of the paper. Blot the painted area with crumpled paper towels. An interesting resist effect should occur.
5. When the fraktur has dried, glue the birth certificate to construction paper.

Variations
1. *Manila Paper:* Substitute manila paper for drawing paper, and eliminate the tempera resist technique.
2. *Color:* After drawing the design with pencil, carefully paint the shapes with tempera. Outline the design, and print the information with a black marking pen after the paint has dried.

Fraktur Design Birth Certificate:
Sample Designs

Fraktur Design Birth Certificate:
Sample Designs *(cont.)*

60

Sgraffito Plates

*H*istorically, the sgraffito technique originated in Europe and was adapted by American colonial craftsmen. Because colored glazes where not always available, this technique allowed white ceramic to obtain a red color for the design.

Decorative earthenware plates where created from round slabs of red clay. The surface of the red clay plates was coated with a layer of gray slip (softened gray clay with the consistency of pudding). A design was scratched through the surface of the slip and into the slab revealing the red clay underneath the gray coating. After the clay piece dried, it was fired in a kiln. The heat turned the gray slip to white while the red carved lines remained. Pottery objects such as bowls, pitchers, and plates were decorated in this manner. A special gift for weddings or the birth of a child was a plate decorated especially for the occasion.

Materials:

- ❏ scrap paper
- ❏ rolling pin
- ❏ toothpicks
- ❏ gray clay slip
- ❏ red clay
- ❏ water bowl
- ❏ ribbon
- ❏ pencils
- ❏ plastic knife
- ❏ 2" (5 cm) wide paintbrushes
- ❏ plastic coffee can lid
- ❏ large nails or old pencils
- ❏ sample designs (pages 59-60)
- ❏ kiln*

Procedures:

1. Draw a Pennsylvania Dutch design for the plate. Use the sample fraktur designs on pages 59 and 60 for ideas.
2. Roll out the red clay to ½" (1.25 cm) thickness.
3. Push the lid on the surface of the clay and cut around the circle with the knife.
4. Smooth the edges of the clay slab with water. Poke two holes near the outside edge. These will be used to hang the plate.
5. Paint the slip onto the surface of the red plate with the wide paintbrush. Two or three coats of slip may be needed. Let the slip dry in between applications.
6. With a toothpick, carefully draw the design into the surface of the slip.
7. If the design was successfully drawn with the toothpick, go over the lines heavily with a nail or an old pencil. This will reveal the red clay underneath.
8. If a mistake occurs, brush over the design with another layer of slip.
9. When the plate has dried for about a week, fire it in a kiln. String it with ribbon and hang.

Variations:

1. *Ruffled Edge:* Before slip is applied to the surface of the clay, press your thumb around the edge of the clay circle to create a decorative ruffled edge.
2. *Personalization:* A name and birth year may be incorporated into the plate design.

*Note: This activity does require firing in a kiln. Natural drying will not produce the same effect.

Bargello Needlepoint

*N*eedlepoint is embroidery on woven canvas. It began as a creative pastime in Elizabethan England. This needlecraft was used to create pictures as well as to decorate fabric and fashion accessories. In Colonial America, bargello needlepoint flourished in New England and was typically used to create upholstery fabric.

Bargello is a type of needlepoint based on straight up and down stitches that vary in length. The progressive steps form a repeating zigzag pattern. Bargello is sometimes called Florentine Embroidery or Hungarian Point. It is also known as Flame Stitch because of the distinct zigzag pattern created by the stitches.

The bargello pattern is easily designed and plotted on graph paper. The first row is designed with peaks; the succeeding rows copy the first. The pattern is then created with yarn in an open-weave fabric canvas.

Materials:

- ❏ graph paper (4 squares per inch or approx. 2 per cm)
- ❏ crayons
- ❏ thin yarn (3 colors or more)
- ❏ tapestry needles
- ❏ pencil
- ❏ plastic needlepoint canvas
- ❏ scissors

Procedures:

1. Start developing a bargello pattern about 2" (5 cm) from the top of the graph paper. Use pencil to color in the appropriate number of vertical squares. The pattern should resemble up-and-down steps that form peaks. (Refer to the illustration.) **Note:** The number of squares colored in a vertical row will determine the *length* of the stitch. Rows should not be shorter than 3 squares high or taller than 7 squares.

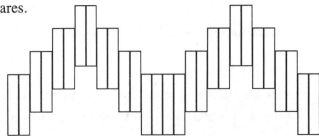

2. After the first row is designed all the way across the graph paper, use crayon to copy the succeeding rows to develop a color scheme.

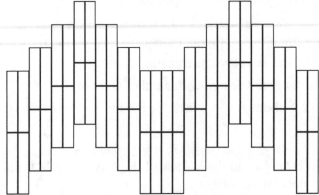

3. After the design is created in color on the graph paper, begin stitching the design on the plastic canvas with yarn. Be careful to follow the pattern and count the appropriate number of squares.

Barn Hex Symbols

*A*nother popular folk art of the Pennsylvania Germans was creating barn hex symbols. These good luck symbols were painted on the front and back ends of barns as well as over the front door of a newly married couple. Hex symbols first appeared in America in the 1800's. In Europe, early versions of these decorated disks were traditionally painted over doorways and gates.

Usually three to seven disks were painted with a star motif in the center. These star symbols represented good luck, fertility, guardianship against evil, and protection from lightning. Center stars had four or more points. Around the edges of the circles, straight lines or geometric shapes were painted. Additional good luck symbols incorporated other motifs of Pennsylvania Dutch design, such as hearts, birds, and tulips.

 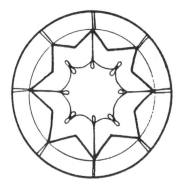 

Materials:
- ❑ compass or round plastic lids
- ❑ pencil
- ❑ scissors
- ❑ glue
- ❑ paper
- ❑ crayons
- ❑ cardboard
- ❑ sample designs (page 63)

Procedures:
1. Draw a large circle with the compass or around the lid.
2. Draw a hex design in the center of the circle. You can model it after a design on this page or make up your own.
3. Add geometric lines and shapes around the edges.
4. Color the design using four colors.
5. Cut out the hex symbol and glue it to cardboard, making it sturdy.

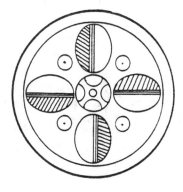  

Corn Husk Dolls

A popular dollmaking technique from early Colonial days is the corn husk doll. Toys were not considered a necessary item for life in the New World by early pilgrims. Elaborate dolls from Europe were expensive and not easily obtainable at that time. Children often used walnuts or carved dried apples for dolls' heads. Bodies were made from old cloth. It is believed that Indians taught pilgrim children how to use corn husks to make these simple dolls.

Materials:

- ❑ 7 corn husks
- ❑ scissors
- ❑ string or yarn
- ❑ large bowl of water

Procedures for a Female or Male Doll:

1. Soak corn husks in water until pliable.
2. Cut the yarn into 4" (10 cm) lengths.
3. Roll one husk into a tight ball.
4. Place the ball into the center of a second corn husk; cover and fold in half over the ball and tie securely under the ball. This will be the head and neck piece. Set aside.

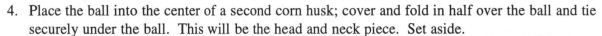

5. Roll a corn husk along the width to form a tube. Tie each end with yarn. This tube will become both arms. Set aside.

6. Hold onto the neck. Place two additional husks, pointed ends down, on top of the head, and two more behind the head.

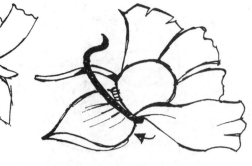

7. Tie yarn securely on top of the first string used to tie the head.

64

Corn Husk Dolls (cont.)

8. Hold the doll by the neck, and carefully fold down the four corn husks.

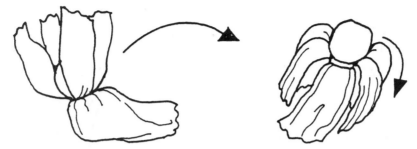

9. Decide which side will be the face. Slip the arms under the two husks that are under the head. Tie below the arms to make the chest and waist.

10a. **For a female doll:** gently fluff out the skirt.

10b. **For a male doll:** cut husks of skirt up to 1" (2.5 cm) below the waist to create two leg bundles. Tie at the bottom of each leg.

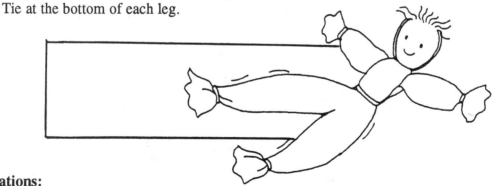

Variations:

1. *Bent Arms:* Bend arms at the elbow and pin into the chest. When the doll is dry, remove the pin. Arms will remain in a bent position.

2. *Hair:* Yarn or corn silk may be glued on for hair. Bandannas or scarves from bits of fabric may be tied onto the head and waist.

Quilling

*T*he art of quilling, sometimes called paper filigree, is the technique of creating designs with narrow strips of paper that have been rolled, shaped, arranged, and then affixed onto a background. Quilling began in fifteenth century Italy, where it was used by nuns to decorate around statues. Over the next two centuries, the craft spread to other parts of Europe and eventually to the American colonies. In America, quilling was used to decorate candle sconces, shadow boxes, mirrors, and screens. Historically, the narrow paper strips were tightly wrapped around the quill of a feather to produce the curled shapes.

Materials:
- ❑ cardboard covered with waxed paper
- ❑ narrow strips of paper in various colors
- ❑ white glue
- ❑ straight pins
- ❑ pencils
- ❑ toothpicks
- ❑ basic quilling rolls (page 66)
- ❑ sample designs (page 67)

Procedures:
1. Choose your design from those on page 67, or design your own.
2. Moisten the end of a strip of paper and begin to roll it around a pencil.
3. Carefully slide the paper roll off the pencil and gently bend it into the desired scroll shape. (See basic rolls below.)
4. Make several of each desired shape. Assemble the rolls together, using small amounts of glue applied with a toothpick. Work on top of the waxed paper, and use pins to hold the design in place while drying.
5. Shapes of smaller sizes or different colors may be glued inside larger shapes.
6. Students may try bird, fruit, or insect shapes. Designs may be imaginative or depict specific objects. When the designs have dried, they may be glued onto a background paper or hung as a mobile.

Basic Quilling Rolls:

loose roll

eye

square

triangle

loop

scroll

S shape

V shape

open heart

circle

Quilling: Sample Designs

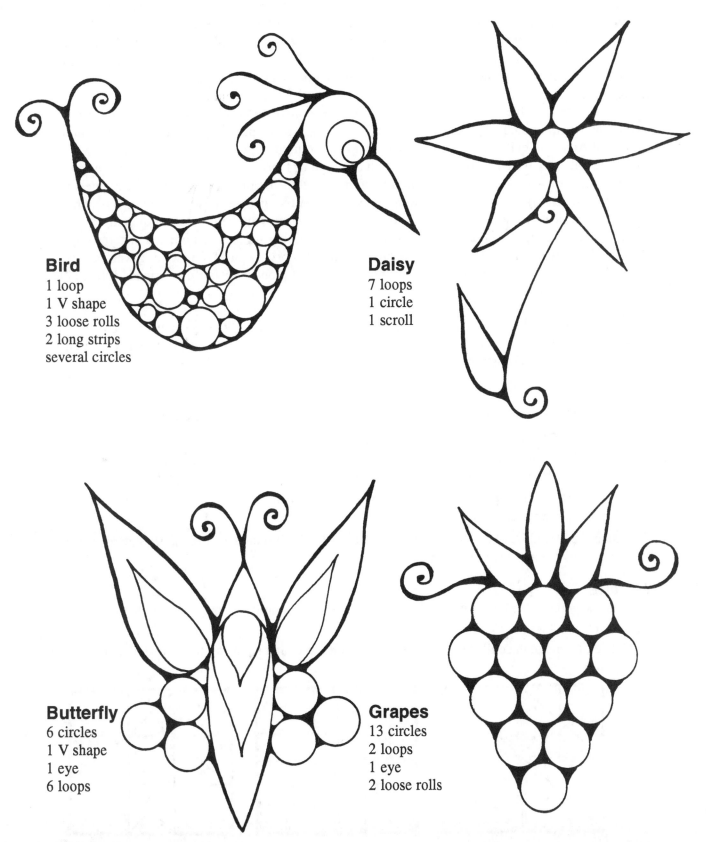

Bird
1 loop
1 V shape
3 loose rolls
2 long strips
several circles

Daisy
7 loops
1 circle
1 scroll

Butterfly
6 circles
1 V shape
1 eye
6 loops

Grapes
13 circles
2 loops
1 eye
2 loose rolls

Quilting

*L*ayers of fabric have been used by man for centuries as a method of protection and insulation for the human body. Early forms of quilting have been traced as far back as the Middle Ages. In Southern Europe, where the weather is relatively mild, quilting was used as a decorative art for clothing. But in Northern Europe, quilting provided protection from the cold weather. It was used extensively in clothing and bed coverings, and the top and back layers were one solid piece of fabric.

Quilting became valuable because of the intricate and decorative embroidery stitches used to fasten together the layers of cloth. Quilts were prized family possessions passed down through generations. In Colonial America, quilts were an important necessity brought over by the pilgrim families. As the quilts wore out, they were carefully patched with any type of fabric that was available. This was the early beginning of American patchwork quilt patterns, developed more extensively in the eighteenth and nineteenth centuries. Early designs were based on repetitive geometric shapes and given symbolic titles. More intricate patterns were floral and animal fabric shapes applied on top of quilted squares. All the layers of fabric were held together by rows of strong, tiny stitches that created patterns on top of the cloth. The patchwork quilt became a record of family history, because old clothing was usually used as the fabric source. It also became an important part of pioneer social life. Friends gathered to socialize and stitch.

Materials: glue, scissors, pencil, ruler, geometric shapes to trace, 12" (30 cm) square of red or black construction paper, 10" (25 cm) square of red or black construction paper, 6" x 9" (15 cm x 22.5 cm) blue, yellow, and white construction paper, sample designs (page 69)

Procedures:
1. Fold the 10" (25 cm) square paper into four, square-shaped quarters. Unfold and flatten.
2. Review and choose from the samples on page 69, or design your own.
3. Draw and cut out basic geometric shapes from each of the other papers to make your design. (For example, cut out four blue circles, four white squares, and four yellow triangles.)
3. Arrange the shapes to create the same design or an alternating design on each section of the 10" (25 cm) square paper. Glue in place.
4. Center the 10" (25 cm) quilt square on top of the 12" (30 cm) construction paper square. Glue in place. This creates one quilt square.

Suggestions:
1. Staple several of the completed quilt squares together on a bulletin board, or glue them to a long length of butcher paper.
2. Use felt to create the quilt. Glue the felt shapes on top of felt squares. Sew the quilt squares together.

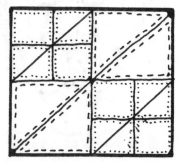 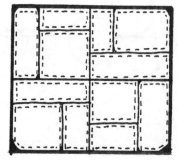 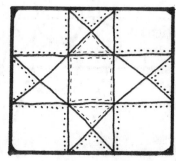

Quilting: Sample Designs

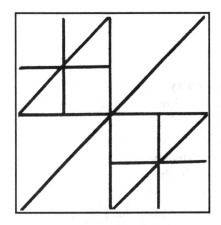

Flock of Geese

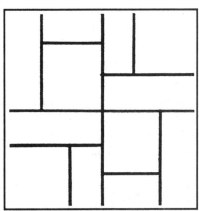

Patience Corner

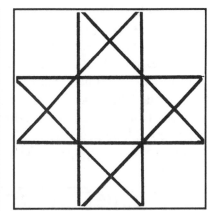

Ohio Star

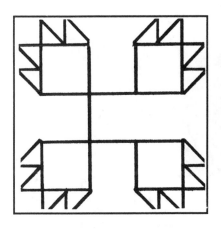

Bear Tracks

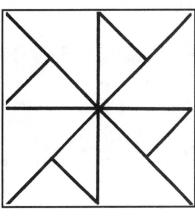

Windmill

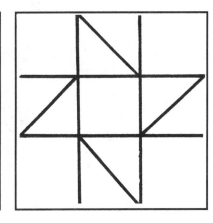

Friendship Star

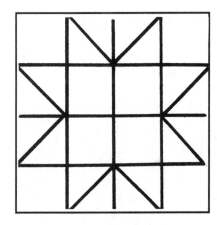

Lone Star

Geese to the Moon

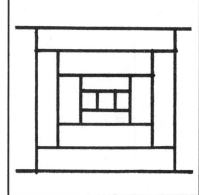

Log Cabin

Art of Ancient Civilizations

*T*he unifying link among the cultures of ancient civilizations cannot be found in style, expression, media, subject, or any of those things which normally identify a cultural expression. What they have in common is much simpler than that: their antiquity. Yet the cultures themselves were not simple. Many were highly developed and advanced in the arts, sciences, mathematics, and so forth. Egyptian pyramids still astound the modern viewer, Incan jewelry delights contemporary craftsmen, and Greek temples attract visitors from all over the world. We enjoy the beauty of the work not just for its historical component, but for the skill and beauty evident in every line. We are amazed because such wonders have been created in times we consider much less advanced than ours. Scholars know, however, that many ancient civilizations were advanced in ways that do great credit to their intelligence, insight, and creativity. History has much to teach us, and through the preservation of such ancient works of art, much to show us as well.

Activities

○ **Clay Mosaics**

○ **Greek/Roman Amphora Vases**

○ **Greek Architecture**

○ **Byzantine Architecture**

○ **Egyptian Cartouche**

○ **Royal Incan Litter**

○ **Islamic Spanish Tile**

Clay Mosaics

*M*osaic is a method used to decorate a surface by covering it with closely set pieces of material, such as glass, tile, shell, and stone. Many cultures have added to the intricate art of mosaic, but most styles have similar origins. The Greeks developed the use of pebble mosaic, which led to the invention of the *tesserae* technique. In Latin, tesserae means *cubes*. This method involves the cutting of stones to fit closely together in a grid. The Romans were noted for the development of such pictorial mosaics, and they are credited with the first use of gold tesserae. Among the largest tesserae scenes is "The Battle of Issus," found in Pompeii and measuring 12' x 20' (3.6 m x 6 m).

Byzantine mosaics formed a continuous skin that covered the walls. The best example is found in the church of Hagia Sophia in Istanbul. Indians of Pre-Columbian Central America used valuable gems and stones to create mosaics on objects. Ceremonial items were covered with jade, garnet, mother-of-pearl, and other precious materials. Masks and knife handles were usually covered with turquoise, the most popular mosaic material.

The intricate art of mosaic can be simulated creatively through clay. By examining examples of mosaic design created by ancient civilizations, students will be able to adapt their own ideas. Have students research to compare and analyze mosaics from Greek, Roman, Byzantine, and Aztec cultures. Also examine computer-generated digital pictures if available, and compare them with the students' designs.

Materials:

- ❑ gray clay
- ❑ graph paper
- ❑ rolling pin
- ❑ newspaper
- ❑ pencil
- ❑ acrylic paint
- ❑ small paintbrushes or cotton-tipped applicator sticks
- ❑ 12" x 12" (30 cm x 30 cm) hardware cloth (wire screen) with ¼" (.5 cm) holes
- ❑ kiln (if firing is desired)

Procedures:

1. Display and discuss examples of mosaic art created by various ancient civilizations.

2. Using graph paper, plan the design by coloring in the appropriate squares. **Note:** Partial squares should not be used as part of the design.

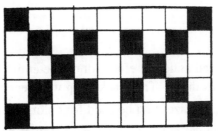

3. Cut a clay slab and lay it on top of the newspaper.

4. Use the rolling pin to flatten out a clay slab approximately ⅜" (1 cm) in thickness and 7" x 9" (18 cm x 23 cm) in size.

Clay Mosaics *(cont.)*

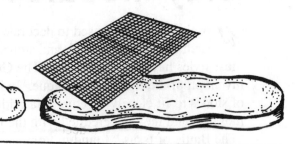

5. Lay the wire screen on top of the clay slab. Use the rolling pin to apply even pressure on top of the screen.

6. Carefully lift off the wire screen. Precise squares will be pressed into the clay.

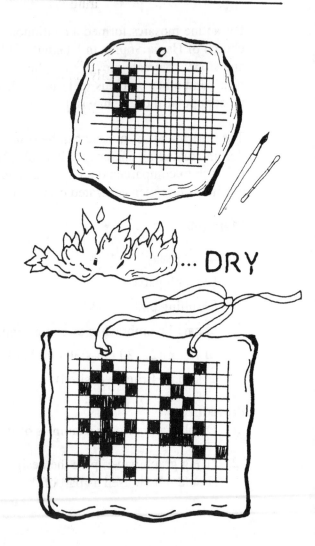

7. Poke holes near the top edge of the slab. These will be used to hang the completed mosaic.

8. Let the slab dry and then fire in a kiln.

9. Use small paintbrushes or cotton-tipped applicators to apply the acrylic paint. Color the appropriate square "tiles" to correspond with the design on the graph paper.

10. Insert ribbon or yarn through the holes to hang the finished mosaic.

Variations:

1. *Antiquing:* For an antiqued effect, dunk the entire slab into diluted black tempera paint after the acrylic paint has dried. The black stain will penetrate into crevices and cracks.

2. *Glazes:* Ceramic glazes can be used for color, but this may require a second kiln firing.

3. *Red Clay:* Softened red clay, the consistency of pudding, can also be used as paint. Apply before the slab is fired.

Greek/Roman Amphora Vases

*A*n amphora is a two-handled vase with a neck narrower than the body. This style of vase has been traced back to Mycenian pottery from the 14th century B.C. They were made in great numbers, and used for storage of grain, olives, wine, oil, and water. Vase heights ranged from one to five feet (30 cm to 1.5 m). The most popular amphora were eighteen inches (45 cm) in height. Wide-mouth vases were painted with black designs, filled with oil, and given away as prizes during the Panathenaic Festivals in Greece. Tall, decorated amphorae were used as burial markers. A triple handle style was created in Nola, Italy, during the Roman Empire.

Early Roman and Greek amphorae were made from an orange-red clay. The surface of the vase was highly polished and then painted with black geometric lines. The most popular pattern was the Greek "key" design. Eventually, animal and human figures were added to the designs. Silhouette figures were painted black with incised lines added for detail. Most of the surface area remained red. This method became popular in Rome, but a reverse technique was later developed. Designs on the red vases were outlined in black, and the areas around the figures were covered with black paint. The figures remained red, and details were added in black.

Figures on the amphorae eventually became more realistic and life-like. They were drawn in a scene depicting a story or event. Often, wives of important soldiers commissioned an amphora to commemorate a battle. Scenes about Greek or Roman gods and athletic events were also popular themes. Historians have been able to learn about specific periods of Greek and Roman civilizations because of the survival of many amphora vases.

Materials:
- ❏ 9" x 12" (22.5 cm x 30 cm) drawing paper
- ❏ scissors
- ❏ rolling pin
- ❏ plastic knife
- ❏ newspaper to cover work area
- ❏ kiln (if firing is desired)
- ❏ pencil,
- ❏ red clay,
- ❏ toothpicks
- ❏ water bowl
- ❏ sample designs (page 74)

Procedures:
1. Fold the paper in half lengthwise.
2. Draw half of a large amphora. Cut out the shape.
3. Flatten the clay into a slab with the rolling pin.
4. Lay the amphora pattern on top of the clay and cut around the shape with the knife.
5. Remove excess clay and smooth the edges of the amphora with water.
6. Use a toothpick to carve lines, patterns, or figures into the clay. Additional shapes may be added with clay. (See page 74.)
7. After the clay has dried for about a week, fire in a kiln.
8. Areas may be painted with black paint, if desired.

Variations:
1. *Paper:* Create an amphora from construction paper. Decorate with marking pens, chalk, or crayons. Glue a folded rectangle to the back to make it stand.
2. *Three-Dimensional Vase:* Use self-hardening clay over small bottles. Add handles and decorate with incised lines and paint.

Greek/Roman Amphora Vases: Sample Designs

Greek Architecture

*B*eginning in the sixth century B.C., Greece was controlled by a succession of dictators. However, eventually it became governed by groups of citizens. Because of this, there was no need for elaborate palaces or large buildings exclusive to royalty. Beautiful architecture was instead preserved for public buildings or temples. Because of the development of arithmetic and geometry in ancient Greece, ratio and proportion were important elements in architecture. The original Greek definition of arithmetic was "to create enjoyment from numbers."

The basic structures of architecture used around the world during this time were the post and lintel: two vertical beams supporting a horizontal crossbeam. In Greece, this structure was greatly refined in proportion and style. The basic structure consisted of a rectangular building surrounded by posts which supported the roof. The posts were designed with three sections. The base was the bottom support, the column was tall and thick, and the capital was the top section which supported the roof. One of three basic styles were used for the buildings. The styles were named after the type of capital on top of the column. The Doric was a simple rectangle, the Ionic was a double spiral and the Corinthian was decorated with carved acanthus leaves.

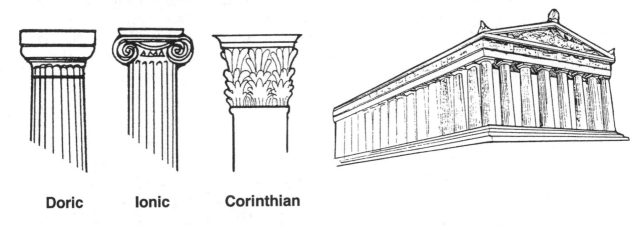

Doric   **Ionic**   **Corinthian**

Materials:

- ❑ pencil
- ❑ scissors
- ❑ plastic knife
- ❑ toothpick
- ❑ 6" x 9" (15 cm x 23 cm) scrap paper
- ❑ clay
- ❑ rolling pin
- ❑ water bowl
- ❑ kiln (if firing is desired)
- ❑ newspaper to cover work area
- ❑ column designs (above)

Procedures:

1. Draw the front of a Greek building on the scrap paper. Cut out the building shape.
2. Roll clay into a flat slab about 6" x 9" (15 cm x 23 cm) and ½" (1.25 cm) thick.
3. Trace the paper building shape on the clay with a toothpick.
4. Cut out the clay shape with the plastic knife. Be careful when cutting away any interior pieces.
5. Smooth the edges of the clay with water.
6. Draw incised lines and spaces into the clay with the toothpick. If a mistake occurs, rub the surface of the clay gently to erase the line.
7. Let the clay dry for about a week before it is fired in a kiln.

Byzantine Architecture

*B*yzantine architecture is the blending of Roman engineering styles with influences from Persia. Domes on small buildings first appeared on round huts or tombs in ancient India, the Near East, and the Mediterranean region. Early Roman technology developed large dome vaults. Byzantine architects perfected a technique of raising domes high on columns.

When the Roman Emperor Constantine began planning his new capital city of Constantinople, now Istanbul, Turkey, he used a majority of Roman architects. Because the city was so close to Asia Minor, styles were also adapted from Islamic influences. In their design, the architects incorporated arches, domes, and open spaces. The most impressive of all buildings were churches built during the fourth century. The basic plan consisted of a dome supported by four columns forming a square. At each side of the square there would be a room opening to the center area. Occasionally columns would be added on one side to extend the structure. Smaller domes also might be built on the east and west roofs. Structures were based on the square, which symbolized harmony with the heavens. The dome represented universal power, and the tower represented ultimate power.

By the sixth century, the world extending from the Mediterranean to India was artistically linked in design ideas, decorative motifs, and structural styles. Mosques and palace structures in Syria, Palestine, Iran, and Iraq were elaborately constructed with domes, towers, and many interior columns and arches. Minarets, which mean "beacons" in Arabic, were small domes supported by tall towers. They were first designed by the Romans as watchtowers.

Materials:

- ❑ 12" x 18" (30 cm x 45 cm) drawing paper
- ❑ pencil
- ❑ crayons
- ❑ rulers
- ❑ protractor
- ❑ watercolors
- ❑ paintbrushes
- ❑ water bowl
- ❑ structure designs (above)

Procedures:

1. Design a Byzantine or Islamic style structure.
2. Draw the architecture using the protractor and ruler.
3. Wet the entire sky area of the picture and brush with blue and purple paint, using horizontal strokes. It is important that the paper be wet for this technique.
4. Set the paper aside to dry for about 3 hours.
5. Fill in some areas with color using crayon.
6. Paint any additional areas if desired, or fill in color with crayon.

Egyptian Cartouche

$\mathcal{S}$ ince the discovery of the Rosetta Stone in 1799, there has been a great interest in ancient Egyptian writing. Egyptian hieroglyphics is a picture-based language. Egyptians started using hieroglyphics about 3100 B.C., and writing soon became a well-developed craft. Scribes (Egyptian writers and teachers) were held in high esteem and given great importance.

Scribes wrote on papyrus. With black ink and reeds, Egyptian pupils would copy that writing onto broken bits of pottery. The scribes would correct over any mistakes with red ink. When the students mastered the hieroglyphic techniques, they would be allowed to write on papyrus.

Pictorial symbols represented specific sounds. What made this system confusing was that often the same symbol also represented entire words. For example, the symbol ⌣⌣ meant either the letter "K" or the word "basket." Hieroglyphics are sometimes compared to rebus writing, in which combinations of symbols represent words or phrases. Hieroglyphics are written in rows, and originally they were read from right to left. Scribes were often talented designers and paid attention to how the entire text appeared. Because of this, the scribe would sometimes write the symbols in a row from top to bottom, bottom to top, or left to right. Finished inscriptions looked very decorative. But there are common clues in hieroglyphic writing. Symbols of animals or people are always facing in the direction of the beginning of the row, and each row of symbols is separated by a line drawn underneath the writing. Names of kings, queens, and other important people are enclosed in a *cartouche,* a rectangle with rounded corners. In reading hieroglyphic text, a cartouche is easily recognized. Often a cartouche was carved from stone and used as a royal seal.

Materials:

- ❑ pencil
- ❑ clay
- ❑ toothpick
- ❑ diluted blue tempera paint
- ❑ paintbrushes
- ❑ hieroglyphic pages (pages 78-79)
- ❑ scrap paper
- ❑ plastic knife
- ❑ water bowl
- ❑ gold acrylic paint
- ❑ thin, black yarn
- ❑ kiln (if desired)

Procedures:

1. Write your name in hieroglyphics on scrap paper. (See pages 78-79.)
2. Cut a rectangular piece of clay about 3" (7.5 cm) long, 2" (5 cm) wide, and 1" (2.5 cm) thick. A longer piece may be necessary if there are many hieroglyphics in your name.
3. Smooth the edges with water and poke a hole through the clay.
4. Draw a line around the edge of the rectangle.
5. Turn the clay in a vertical direction with the hole at the top. Use a toothpick to carve the hieroglyphic symbols into the clay. Do so carefully.
6. After they have dried for about a week, fire the clay pieces in a kiln.
7. Dip the cartouche in diluted blue tempera paint. When dry, paint the edges with gold paint.
8. String yarn through the hole in the cartouche and wear as a pendant.

Egyptian Cartouche: Hieroglyphics

Hieroglyph	Represents	Sound
	vulture	a
	foot	b
	hand	d
	horned snake	f
	shelter	h
	snake	j
	lion	l
	water	n
	hillside	qu
	folded cloth	s
	loaf	t
	reed with baby quail	u
	horned snake	v

Hieroglyph	Represents	Sound
	arm and hand	a
	rope	ch
	reed leaves	ee and y
	stand	g
	reed leaf	i
	basket	k
	owl	m
	mat	p
	mouth	r
	pool	sh
	baby quail	w or oo
	basket with folded cloth	x
	door bolt	z

Egyptian Cartouche:
Hieroglyphics *(cont.)*

ankh
(life)

wedja
(prosperity)

seneb
(health)

neb
(everyone)

per
(house)

mes
(born)

sa
(guardian)

weser
(powerful)

men
(remain)

shen
(protection)

Cleopatra
(Egyptian queen)

Ptolemys
(name of 15 Egyptian kings)

Tutankhamen
(his royal cartouche)

Eye of Horus
(falcon god of the sky, son of Osiris)

Royal Incan Litter

*T*he territory of the Inca civilization covered areas of Ecuador, Peru, Bolivia, Chile, and Argentina. The Incas and their followers moved from one settlement to another in search of fertile land to sustain the people. Neighboring tribes were conquered, and their lands were taken.

The Lord Inca rarely walked, but was carried on a wooden litter decorated in gold. An overhead canopy was covered in leaves encrusted with jewels and trimmed with a fringe made of short gold tubes with red tassels. Symbols for Inti, the Inca sun god (who appears with a human face surrounded by radiating spokes of light), were also part of the design on the litter.

Materials: 7" (17.5 cm) square brown construction paper, 4" (10 cm) green paper, 8 craft sticks, scissors, glue, pencil, ruler, red yarn, gold glitter, marking pens, scraps of colored paper

Procedures:

1. Fold the square brown paper in half twice in the same direction. Unfold and flatten the paper. In the opposite direction, fold the paper in half twice. Unfold and flatten the paper. This should make 16 squares within the 7" (18 cm) square.

2. Cut off one row of squares along the width and length of the paper. Nine squares within a 6" (15 cm) square should remain.

3. Cut four slits as illustrated.

4. Fold up and glue squares A and C on top of square B. Fold up and glue squares D and F on top of square E. You will now have a box without a top. If you wish to make a lower litter, cut the sides down lower on the two sides without folds or on all four sides.

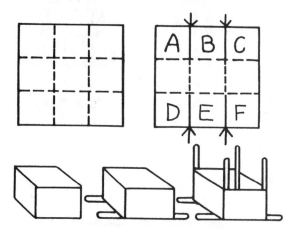

5. Draw Inti, the sun god, on the litter with a marking pen. Add dots of glue and cover with glitter to represent jewels.

6. Glue 4 craft sticks to the bottom of the litter structure to represent carrying handles.

7. Glue a craft stick upright into each corner to hold the canopy. Set aside to dry.

8. Fold the 4" (10 cm) square green paper diagonally in both directions to form 4 triangles. In two opposing sides, cut slits up from the bottom of the triangle almost to the center point. Overlap the flaps and glue in place. This will create the canopy, which is almost rectangular in shape from an aerial view.

9. Decorate the surface by cutting and gluing small leaf and flower shapes to the top. Trim the edges with red yarn. Add some glitter dots.

10. Glue the canopy on top of the upright craft sticks.

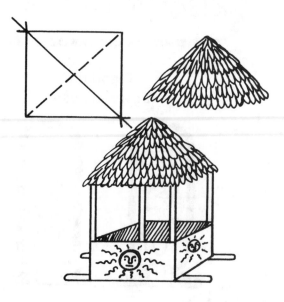

Islamic Spanish Tile

*M*uslims from North Africa invaded Spain in the eighth century. They brought with them a rich heritage of design and pattern. This was most obvious in their building style and architectural decoration. An important type of Islamic art in Spain was ceramics, and the most outstanding example remains their mosaic tile designs. Lustre glazing was first developed in Iraq. This technique gave clay surfaces a shiny appearance. The tiles were decorated with a combination of geometric and floral designs and interlacing stems. Tiles often had a plain or patterned border. Painted glaze designs also included inscriptions of proverbs in calligraphy. Popular were geometric shapes which produced kaleidoscope-type patterns when the tiles were placed together. All shades and variations of blue where most characteristic.

Materials:

- ❏ 12" (30 cm) square black construction paper
- ❏ yellow paper 4 ½" (11.25 cm) square
- ❏ four sheets white paper 4 ½" (11.25 cm) square
- ❏ scissors
- ❏ glue
- ❏ pencil
- ❏ crayons

Procedures:

1. Fold the yellow square in half on the diagonal.
2. Draw a wavy line along one edge, as illustrated.
3. Keep the paper folded, and cut on this line.
4. Open the paper, and draw an X to indicate the bottom corner.
5. Place this shape on top of a white square and trace around the yellow pattern. Repeat this procedure on each of the other 3 white squares.
6. Refold the yellow shape and draw another type of line near the wavy cut edge. Cut on this line to create a new edge on the yellow paper.
7. Place this shape on top of each white square, and trace around the edges. There should now be two lines drawn on each square.
8. Repeat step #6, and trace this shape on top of each white square.
9. Each white square should look identical. There should be three varied lines and four spaces.
10. Color each square the same, using only three colors.
11. Arrange and glue to the black square.

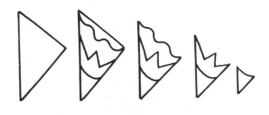

Art of Other Cultures

*G*athered in this section are six engaging activities from cultures as diverse as the opposing ends of the earth. The Philippines, Italy, New Guinea, Panama, Russia, and France are each represented. The craft from each is unique, bearing no similarity to any of the others in subject, media, style, or creativity. Of interest, then, is the fact that no craft amongst these stands out as superior. Each is engaging, each is culturally rich, and each causes the viewer to respond, "Now, isn't that interesting?" Lest students begin to think that "multicultural" is a term that includes only specific cultures, these activities will show them differently.

Activities

○ **Philippine Sarimanok**

○ **Italian Renaissance Rooster Pitcher**

○ **New Guinea Tablet Figures**

○ **Panamanian Mola**

○ **Russian Matryoshka Dolls**

○ **French Jumping Dolls**

Philippine Sarimanok

*T*he Sarimanok is a good luck symbol of the Filipino culture, representing love, courage, and free- dom. A Maranaw tribe legend tells of a sultan who used the Sarimanok bird to send messages to his loved one. The messages were contained in a carved wooden fish and carried by the bird in its beak. The bird flew many miles to another island to deliver the messages. Eventually the Sarimanok brought the princess to the sultan, and they were married. Many Filipino tribes have their own version of this legend and have adopted the Sarimanok as an important part of their culture. The design is used to decorate houses, boats, and musical instruments during holiday celebrations and weddings.

Materials:

- ❑ crayons
- ❑ water bowl
- ❑ paintbrush
- ❑ pencil
- ❑ Filipino words below

- ❑ 9" (23 cm) square manilla paper or brown paper bag
- ❑ 12" x 18" (30 cm x 45 cm) construction paper in any desired color
- ❑ diluted brown tempera paint
- ❑ Sarimanok writing (p. 84)

Pride = pagmamalaki *(pug mah mah lah kee)*

Respect = paggalang *(pug gah lung)*

Love = pagmamahal *(pug mah mah hull)*

Sharing = bigayan *(be guy yun)*

Procedures:

1. Carefully tear off the straight edges of the manila paper.

2. Students can draw their own version of the Sarimanok bird and the fish. The total design should be as large as possible. Color the design with a very heavy application of crayon.

3. Carefully print the four Filipino words given above around the bird with crayon. Crumple the entire paper when finished, then uncrumple and flatten out the paper.

4. Gently brush the tempera paint over the entire surface of the paper. The paint will "resist" and not adhere to the oily surface of the crayon.

5. While the paint is drying, have students use page 84 to write a personal statement concerning the meaning of each word. They may choose events, memories, or ambitions about which to write.

6. Glue the dried picture to the top portion of the construction paper. Cut out the writing and glue it below the Sarimanok design.

       TCM #617 MULTICULTURAL ART ACTIVITIES

Philippine Sarimanok: Sample Design and Writing

Pagmamalaki (Pride)

Paggalang (Respect)

Pagmamahal (Love)

Bigayan (Sharing)

84

Italian Renaissance Rooster Pitcher

*T*he good luck rooster pitcher dates back to the Renaissance in the Republic of Florence. The most powerful family at that time was the wealthy Medici family. The rival Pazzi family plotted many times to kill them.

Great amounts of land were owned by the Medicis, and Guiliano d'Medici frequently held festivals in the villages for the many peasants who worked the land. The Pazzi family attempted to have Guiliano killed during one of the festivals in the village of Galliana. The primary occupation of this village was raising chickens. Spies for the Pazzi family drugged Guiliano's wine, and he fell asleep among the chickens. Late at night when the assassins came, they were startled by so many chickens in the courtyard. The noise made by the chickens alarmed Guiliano's guards, who captured the assassins.

Guiliano was so thankful for being saved that he threw another festival. He ordered his craftsmen to create wine and water pitchers in the shape of roosters. These were given to all the people in the village. Traditionally, a rooster pitcher is given in Italy as a housewarming gift, symbolizing protection from evil.

Materials: clay, clay slip, rolling pin, toothpicks, paper clip, plastic knife, newspaper to cover work areas, water bowl, tongue depressor, patterns (page 86), kiln (if firing is desired)

Procedures:

1. Roll out clay into a flat slab about 8" x 11" (20 cm x 28 cm) and ½" (1.25 cm) thick.
2. Place the three pattern pieces on the clay, and cut around them with the knife.
3. Use the toothpick to scratch lines around the edges of the bottom piece and the sides of each rooster, as indicated on the pattern.
4. Smear clay slip on top of the same edges as in step #3.
5. Attach the bottom sides of each rooster body to the oval bottom piece.
6. Repeat steps #3 and #4 to attach the body sections as indicated.
7. Squeeze together the two sides of the body from the head to the beak and down the chest, where they connect to the oval bottom. Squeeze together the tail sections.
8. Use a tongue depressor to press the clay together on the inside of the pitcher.
9. Open the beak with a toothpick.
10. Roll remaining clay into a thick coil handle and attach from the inside.
12. Use a paper clip to press feather shapes into the clay. Decorate the rest of the rooster as desired.
13. After the pitcher has dried for about a week, fire in a kiln. Color with glaze or paint if desired.

Italian Renaissance Rooster Pitcher: Patterns

86

New Guinea Tablet Figures

The New Guinea island of New Ireland is known for malonggan pole carvings and tablets. The carved poles depict individual human figures or several stacked figures. These poles were used inside of huts as roof supports and as part of ceremonial rituals. Tall tablets made from flat wooden boards attached to rods were painted to resemble human forms. Some were created with raised hands holding spears or smaller figures. These tablets were placed outside of homes near the entrance area as guardians against evil.

The long tablets were painted with a large face, horizontal eyebrows, and large eyes. The nose is a large curved shape. The jaw is designed with wide horizontal rectangles having rows of large pointed teeth. Black, white, yellow, and red were used to paint the facial features. Geometric patterns painted in black were used on other sections of the tablet. Decorations were added using shells, stones, bone, fur, cane, fibers, and feathers.

Materials:

- ❏ tongue depressor
- ❏ marking pens
- ❏ scissors
- ❏ optional: raffia, fur, and feathers
- ❏ toothpicks
- ❏ glue
- ❏ paper scraps (black, white, red, and yellow)

Procedures:

1. Glue two toothpicks to one end of the tongue depressor.

2. Turn over the tongue depressor and begin designing the tablet using marking pens and bits of cut paper.

3. Natural materials, such as raffia and feathers, may be added.

4. A spear may be added by using an additional toothpick.

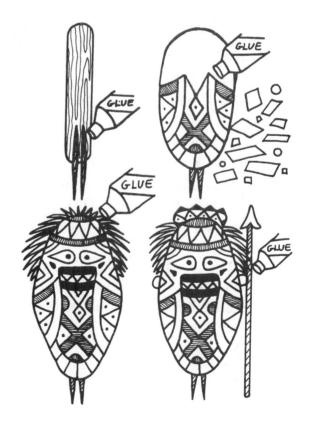

Larger Variation:

To create a large tablet, draw a tall oval shape on brown tagboard. Add designs using construction paper and paint.

Panamanian Mola

*K*una Indian women on the San Blas Islands off Panama developed a unique textile. Molas are fabric pictures created from several layers of colorful cloth. The top layer of rectangular cloth is traditionally black, red, or orange. Three to seven layers of cloth are layered underneath.

Starting with a central figure shape, each layer of cloth is cut away around the shape to reveal other layers underneath. Tiny stitches decorate the entire design and aid in holding the layers of fabric together. This process is often referred to as "reverse applique."

Popular themes of mola textiles are animals, reptiles, flowers, dreams, and tribal superstitions. Early molas were very geometric and had specific meanings and interpretations. These pictures decorated blouses, vests, dresses, and belts.

Materials:

❑ 9" x 12" (23 cm x 30 cm) black, green, yellow, orange, and blue construction paper

❑ scissors

❑ pencil

❑ glue

Procedures:

1. Set aside the black paper.
2. Draw an animal, floral, or reptile shape on another sheet of construction paper. Cut out the shape. Save all paper scraps.
3. Glue this shape on top of another color paper.
4. Cut around the shape leaving about a ⅜" (1 cm) border around it.
5. Glue this two-color shape onto a third sheet of paper.
6. Cut around the two-color shape leaving ⅜" (1 cm) border.
7. Glue the three-color shape on to a fourth color and cut around the edges leaving a ⅜" (1 cm) border.
8. Glue this four-color shape on top of the black construction paper.
9. Cut shapes from the paper scraps and glue around the central shape to create elements of the central shape's habitat.
10. Layer these shapes as above to create the mola effect.

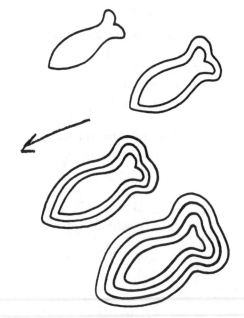

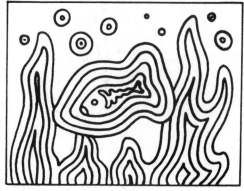

Russian Matryoshka Dolls

atryoshka dolls are hollow wooden doll sets containing smaller nesting dolls inside. Each doll is graduated in size with the smallest fitting neatly inside the next large size. Matryoshka in Russian means "grandmother," and the dolls are traditionally painted wearing a babushka head scarf with large red and yellow flowers. The dolls were hand carved by the grandfather in the family, and they became treasured heirlooms. Large doll sets containing many nesting dolls inside are the most valuable. Other valuable sets contain dolls with the smallest about ½" (1.25 cm) tall.

Materials:

- ❑ pencil
- ❑ glue
- ❑ marking pens
- ❑ sample designs (page 90)
- ❑ construction paper (white, red, yellow, and orange)

- ❑ scissors
- ❑ crayons
- ❑ stapler

Procedures:

1. Cut the white paper to the following dimensions:
   - 12" x 18" (30 cm x 45 cm)
   - 10" x 15" (25 cm x 38 cm)
   - 8" x 12" (20 cm x 30 cm)
   - 6" x 9" (15 cm x 23 cm)

2. Curve each sheet into a tube and glue together. The shortest dimension will be the height of the tube. The circumference of each tube should get smaller as the tubes get shorter. Place the tubes inside of each other to check that they will fit.

3. Cut the red paper to the following dimensions:
   - 6" x 18" (15 cm x 45 cm)
   - 4" x 15" (10 cm x 38 cm)
   - 3" x 12" (7.5 cm x 30 cm)
   - 2" x 9" (5 cm x 23 cm)

4. Fold each red sheet in half, and draw the scarf as illustrated.

5. Cut out each scarf and fit it around the top of each tube. Make adjustments to the scarf by cutting away more paper if necessary.

6. Cut out flowers and leaves from the remaining paper. Glue to the scarf and around the bottom of the doll.

7. Carefully draw a face on each doll.

Russian Matryoshka Dolls:
Sample Designs

90

French Jumping Dolls

F rench jumping dolls *(pantin)* have segmented body parts that jump or move by pulling one string that connects the entire body. Early forms of these two-dimensional dolls have been found in ancient Egypt and Greece. The dolls became very popular and elaborate in the eighth century French court, where they were mainly enjoyed by adults. Famous artists of the time designed and painted these animated stringed figures, and they were valued as collector items. Eventually spreading to other parts of Europe, these dolls were called Hampelmann in Germany and Jumping Jacks in England.

Designs for all types of jumping dolls, representing human or animal figures, were published in popular magazines. Like paper dolls, they were ready to be cut out and strung together. The jumping figures resembled paper dolls, but they were jointed and movable. Strings attached to various joints provided the movement when one central string was pulled. These dolls were usually created from heavy cardboard and richly painted and decorated with gold, lace, fabrics, or feathers.

Materials:

- ❏ 10" (25 cm) square cardboard
- ❏ scissors
- ❏ marking pens
- ❏ small, pronged paper fasteners
- ❏ large bead
- ❏ optional: feathers, sequins, glitter, etc.
- ❏ pencil
- ❏ crayons
- ❏ yarn or string
- ❏ large nail or craft knife
- ❏ patterns (pages 92-93)

Procedures:

1. Trace all the pattern pieces for the basic doll body onto the cardboard. Leave space around each body part. (Or trace the clown patterns and skip steps #2 and #3.)

2. Draw over the traced lines, adding extra areas for a full skirt, wide hat, large shoes, or any other items of clothing. If an animal doll is desired, add a tail, ears, and claws, or draw any necessary changes or additions to the basic pattern.

3. Use marking pens to add details to the body parts and/or clothing.

4. Color and carefully cut out all the pieces, labeling each part on the back side.

5. Attach glitter, feathers, sequins, and so forth with glue.

6. Attach together each body section at the back side of the body with a fastener (indicated with an X on the pattern).

7. String the doll together as illustrated. Knot string at the dots on the arms and thighs.

8. Tie a large bead at the end of the string.

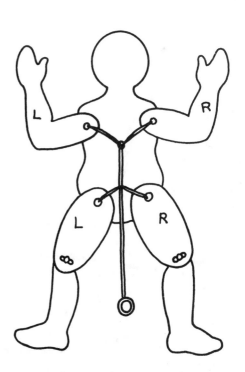

French Jumping Dolls: Basic Pattern

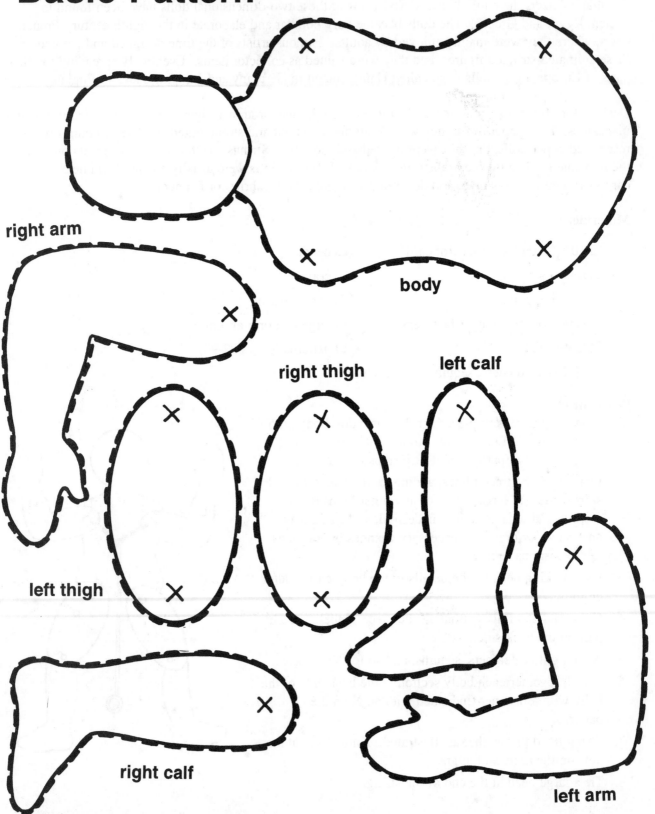

right arm

body

right thigh

left calf

left thigh

right calf

left arm

     92

French Jumping Dolls:
Clown Pattern

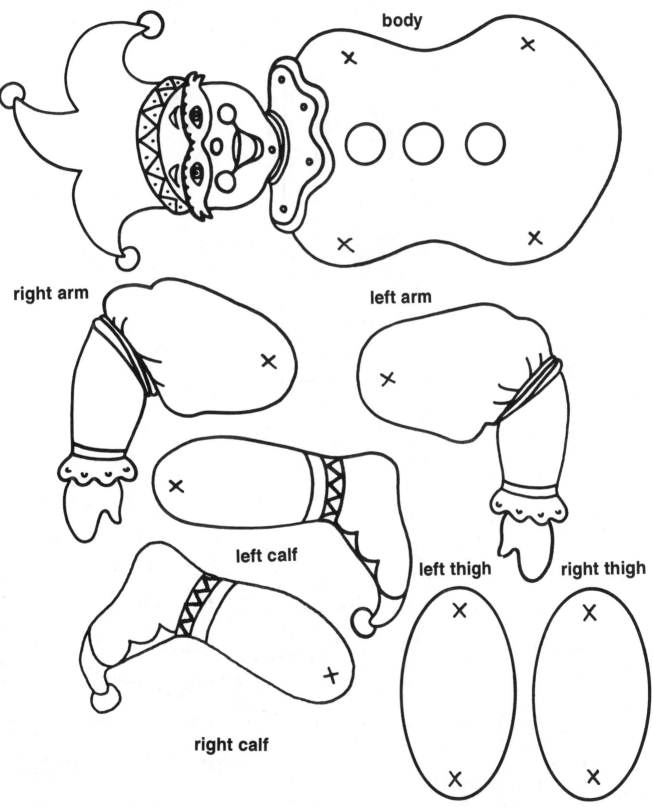

body

right arm

left arm

left calf

left thigh

right thigh

right calf

Using a Kiln

Several activities in this book require the use of a kiln if they are to be done properly. Of course, many schools are not likely to have kilns and/or qualified personnel to operate them. If this is the case in your school, a simple alternative is to go to a nearby ceramic or pottery shop. It is likely that, for a small charge, the proprietors will fire your pieces for you. In so doing, you will also have the comfort of professional handling for your students' works of art.

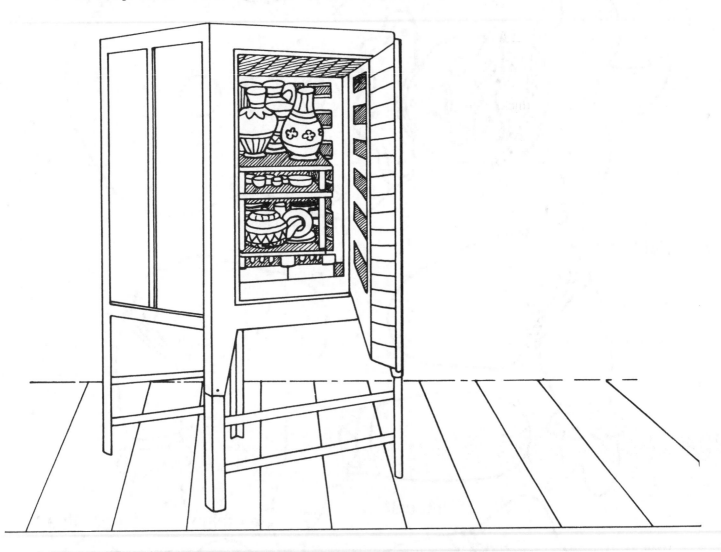

If you will be firing the objects yourself, here are some important things to keep in mind.

1. Dry them completely before firing. This takes about a week. If you do not wait until the objects have dried, they are likely to explode during firing.

2. You can test for dryness prior to firing by holding the object to your skin. If it feels cool, it is not quite dry.

3. You can speed drying by placing the object in the sun, near a heating vent, or by another source of heat. Caution: if the heat source is *too* hot, the object may dry too quickly and crack.

4. Children should never fire objects themselves. This is an adult job. Children attempting it must have qualified adult supervision.

Glossary

Acrylic Paint: a plastic-based paint that adheres to most surfaces.

Acrylic Polymer: a clear plastic liquid that creates a shiny surface when applied.

Ankh: a cross having a looped top; symbolizes life.

Art Elements: color, line, form (shape), space, and texture.

Artifact: an object designed and created by man, usually having a useful purpose.

Block Printing Ink: a thick, high quality ink used in printing.

Brayer: a small roller used to spread ink or paint in a printing process.

Column: a post used to support a roof.

Crayon Resist: see watercolor resist.

Design (verb): to plan an artwork, determining the use of shapes, lines, colors, and textures.

Design (noun): lines, shapes, colors, or textures used to decorate an area.

Decorate: to fill an empty space with planned lines, shapes, or colors.

Diluted Tempera Paint: two cups water mixed with one-half cup tempera paint. Test paint to create desired dilution.

Exterior: the outside of a building or objects.

Eye-Level Line: an imaginary horizontal line that is the base for your field of vision, like the horizon line.

Facade: The exterior design of a building.

Fire: to "bake" dried ceramic clay in a kiln.

Geometric Shapes: shapes based on mathematics having precise linear measurements: square, rectangle, circle, half-circle, crescent, oval, polygon, etc.

Glaze: a paint-like substance used to add color on ceramic artwork; must be fired in a kiln.

Incised Lines: lines that are cut into a surface to create designs.

Interior: the inside of a building or object.

Kiln: a special type of oven used to fire clay; temperature may be regulated to over 2,500 degrees Fahrenheit (1,350 degrees Celsius).

Glossary *(cont.)*

Mosaic: a surface decoration made from small pieces of material, creating a design or picture.

Pattern (verb): to embellish an area with a design of shapes, lines, or color.

Pattern (noun): a shape used as a model to create an object.

Perspective: a drawing technique that creates the illusion of a three-dimensional shape on a two-dimensional surface.

Profile: the side view of a person or figure.

Proportion: relationships of size or amounts of color, line, space, and shapes.

Self-Hardening Clay: a clay substance that eventually dries and hardens at room temperature.

Slip: diluted clay the consistency of thick pudding; used to join clay pieces together or color clay surfaces. Mix two cups water with one-half pound of clay. Add more water if necessary.

Space: the distance around and between shapes.

Raffia: a coarse, natural fiber.

Repetition: a line, shape, or color used over and over to create a pattern.

Roof Line: the top outline edge of a building or series of buildings.

Slab: a flat piece of clay.

Symmetrical: a design or an object in which each half is identical.

Tempera Paint: a water-based paint.

Texture: the surface quality of an object, either real or imitated.

Three-Dimensional: possessing length (or height), width, and depth, as in a cube.

Two-Dimensional: possessing length and width, as in a piece of paper.

Vanishing Point: a specific place on the eye-level line where all objects appear to get smaller as they are drawn closer together.

Watercolor Resist: watercolor paint spread over marks made with crayon. The wax in the crayon will resist the water. Only areas not covered with crayon will absorb the paint.

Watercolor Wash: watercolor paint spread over the entire area of a damp surface.